GW00792152

The Ways of God

'Teach me your way, O Lᴏʀᴅ, and I will walk
in your truth; give me an undivided heart,
that I may fear your name.'
Psalm 86:11

Selwyn Hughes
Revised and updated by Mick Brooks
FURTHER STUDY: IAN SEWTER

© CWR 2012. Dated text previously published as *Every Day
with Jesus: The Ways of God* (Sep/Oct 1987) by CWR. This
edition revised and updated for 2012 by Mick Brooks.
CWR, Waverley Abbey House, Waverley Lane, Farnham, Surrey GU9 8EP, UK
Tel: 01252 784700 Email: mail@cwr.org.uk
Registered Charity No. 294387. Registered Limited Company No. 1990308.

Unless otherwise stated, all Scripture quotations are from the Holy Bible,
New International Version. © International Bible Society.

Cover image: Getty/Photonica/Nick Ballon.
Quiet Time image: sxc.hu/gerard79
Printed in England by Linney Print

MIX
Paper from
responsible sources
www.fsc.org   FSC® C015900

ry Day with Jesus is available in large print from CWR. It is also available on **audio and DAISY**
he UK and Eire for the sole use of those with a visual impairment worse than N12, or who are
stered blind. For details please contact **Torch Trust for the Blind**, Tel: 01858 438260.
ch Trust for the Blind, Torch House, Torch Way, Northampton Road, Market Harborough, LE16 9HL.

A word of introduction ...

It seems incredible that Waverley Abbey House has been open as CWR's headquarters now for 25 years. Each year around 5,500 people come through its doors, just under 4,500 beds are made and approximately 20,000 meals are served. It is a place where marriages have been mended, burned-out leaders have been restored, people have been healed and envisioned, professionals and counsellors have been trained, and many thousands brought to a fresh understanding of and enthusiasm for God's Word. Many have gone on to establish significant ministries of their own both in the UK and around the world.

God's timing never ceases to amaze me, not least in that we find ourselves on this anniversary at yet another milestone - that of a new step for CWR with Pilgrim Hall, which also has a rich Christian heritage and history.

The process of purchasing and developing the ministry at Pilgrim Hall has certainly been one in which the ways of God have been very evident. As Selwyn explores these ways in this issue, I pray that we will see how, when we begin to understand God's ways rather than resist and struggle with them, He will indeed 'reveal, reverse and restore'.

I thank God for all of you who have invested in and continue to invest in the ministry of CWR. First written as a celebratory issue, I hope that this will be so again, as we move into a new phase.

His way is to do everything in His time: may all the glory go to Him.

Sincerely yours, in His name

Mick

Mick Brooks, Consulting Editor

Free small-group resources to accompany this issue can be found at www.cwr.org.uk/extra and you can now join the *EDWJ* conversation on Facebook www.facebook.com/edwjpage

'It's His way'

FOR READING & MEDITATION - EXODUS 33:1-14

'... the LORD would speak to Moses face to face, as a man speaks with his friend.' (v.11)

This issue of *Every Day with Jesus* was originally written to coincide with the official opening in 1987 of Waverley Abbey House, CWR's teaching and training centre. CWR was formed in 1965, and the purchase of the House was a significant milestone in the life of the ministry. And so, at this juncture, it seemed appropriate to ask ourselves: what are some of the lessons we have learnt along the way? How has God revealed Himself to us and what has He shown us about His manner and methods of working?

There is no doubt in my mind that one of the most significant and important lessons that Father God has taught us, and is still teaching us, is a deeper understanding of His ways. The insights He has given us on this matter have now been gathered together to form this issue – *The Ways of God*.

And so we begin with the thought that the more we know and understand God's ways, the better we will know Him. When we meet someone new, we may hear others say of them: 'It is just his way' or, 'He thinks and acts differently to most people, but once you get used to his ways, you will get on well with him'. So it is with God. The better we know and understand His ways, the richer will be our relationship with Him.

Take this verse: 'He made known his ways to Moses, his deeds to the people of Israel' (Psa. 103:7). The Israelites knew only the acts of God and easily fell prey to murmurings and misunderstandings; Moses knew the ways of God and became, as our text for today shows, His confidant and friend. Some see only the *actions* of God: happy are those who understand His *ways*.

FURTHER STUDY

Gen. 18:16-33;
James 2:21-23

1. Why would God hide or reveal His plans?

2. What was special about Abraham?

O God, I see that if I am to get on with You better then I must come to know and understand Your ways. Open my eyes that I may see, not just Your acts, but the purposes that lie behind those acts. In Jesus' name. Amen.

The leisured heart

FOR READING & MEDITATION – PROVERBS 3:1-18

'Her ways are pleasant ways, and all her paths are peace.' (v.17)

The amazing thing about knowing and understanding the ways of God is that it has helped me to look at my difficulties and circumstances through a different lens, and everything has taken on a completely new perspective. Life can change from boredom and emptiness, profitlessness and purposelessness, to meaning, direction, hope, encouragement and deliverance from despair.

As I look back to the early days of CWR and reflect on God's leadings, I clearly remember some situations when I was at the point of panic – simply because I did not know or understand the ways of God. I used to say to myself: 'What is God doing? Why doesn't He do this, rather than that? What possible purpose can He have in taking us down this road?' If I had had a better understanding of the ways of God and had known them as well as I do today, many difficult situations would have been robbed of their fear. I saw His *acts*, but did not understand His *ways*.

I have now a little more understanding and insight into the way God works and, as I came to terms with it, so I entered into the experience of what someone has described as 'the leisured heart'. Those who knew me well said: 'What has changed you? You were fussy, aggressive and easily ruffled – what has made the difference?' I was able to share with them that I had begun to understand something of God's ways, and with that understanding had come a deep inner security and peace. Many people are living strained spiritual lives, and though there can be *many* reasons for this, by far the commonest is this – we are unfamiliar with our Father's ways.

FURTHER STUDY

Exod. 14:10-14;
Isa. 26:1-4

1. Contrast Moses and the people.

2. Who enjoys perfect peace?

My Father and my God, I know to understand Your ways is something that is important and significant. I need also to become more familiar with You. Help me come through to a deeper and clearer understanding of this. For Jesus' sake. Amen.

'Will you be made whole?'

FOR READING & MEDITATION – JOHN 5:1-15

'When Jesus saw him lying there ... he asked him,
"Do you want to get well?"' (v.6)

We ended yesterday by saying that some are living strained spiritual lives because they do not always understand their Father's ways. So they find it difficult to know the experience of the 'leisured heart'.

Jesus, of course, is our example of what it means to live in the knowledge and understanding of the Father's ways. He was never in a hurry, and appeared to be adequate for every situation that confronted Him. In the passage before us today, we see He was so familiar with His Father's ways that He quietly walked past the crowd of desperate people sitting by the pool of Bethesda and said to just one person: 'Do you want to be made well?' Why didn't He ask that same question of everyone? There was a great crowd of people needing His help – why focus on just one?

I used to have great difficulty with this passage until I came to see the connecting links in verses 17 and 19: 'My Father is always at his work ... and I too am working ... the Son can do nothing by himself; he can do only what he sees his Father doing ...' Jesus seems to be saying that He did not get His guidance from what went on around Him, but from what went on above Him. Note the phrase – 'what he sees his Father doing'. Jesus looked up to heaven, saw that His Father's way in this situation was not to heal all but to heal one, then moved in to make the divine will a reality. The way of man would be to minister to the whole crowd, but God's way was to single out one individual and focus only on him. We cannot say why, but a closer look at God's character reveals His motives are always good.

FURTHER STUDY

John 5:17-30;
15:1-5;
2 Tim. 2:1-4

1. What did Jesus seek?

2. What should we seek?

Father, help me to understand that though Your ways sometimes seem unpredictable, they are never capricious. There is always a good, gracious and benevolent reason behind everything You do. Amen.

Is God Irish?

FOR READING & MEDITATION – ISAIAH 55:1-13

'As the heavens are higher than the earth, so are my ways higher than your ways and my thoughts than your thoughts.' (v.9)

The incident we looked at yesterday illustrates the fact that God's ways are so different from man's that they sometimes appear to be the complete opposite. We have a certain approach to life – but God has another. And unless we come to terms with this, we will find a lot of the things that go on in our Christian life make no sense at all. A friend of mine from Northern Ireland claims he can prove from the Bible that God is Irish. When asked to support this claim, he says: 'Because God does everything in the opposite way to everyone else!'

FURTHER STUDY

2 Kings 6:8-23;
Matt. 5:43-48

1. How was the king of Israel's thinking different from God's?

2. How did Jesus reveal God's 'Irish' nature?

We may have a fixed view and modus operandi to life – but God who understands and sees all may have another. For example, we might think that leadership is getting others to serve us. However, God says: 'Whoever wants to become great among you must be your servant' (Matt. 20:26). The great are not those who have the greatest number of servants, but those who serve the greatest number. Then again – man thinks that to surrender his life to God is to lose it. God says otherwise: 'For whoever wants to save his life will lose it, but whoever loses his life for me will find it' (Matt. 16:25).

Take one more example – we think that the basic keys to good health are sleep, food, exercise and rest. A phrase often used in newspapers and magazines is this: 'You are what you eat.' God says that '... godliness has value for all things ...' (1 Tim. 4:8). Sleep, food, exercise and rest are important, but not nearly as important as a godly lifestyle. It is not so much what you eat but what is eating you that is important.

O Father, I am beginning to understand that my ways are not always Yours. Help me bring my wandering desires and inclinations into line with Your perfect will. In Jesus' name I pray. Amen.

CWR Ministry Events
PLEASE PRAY FOR THE TEAM

te	Event	Place	Presenter(s)
p	Insight into Bereavement	Waverley Abbey House	Peter Jackson
ep	Discovering Your Spiritual Gifts	WAH	Andy Peck
ep	Insight into Depression	Pilgrim Hall	Chris Ledger
ep	Discovering More About God's Story	WAH	Philip Greenslade
ep	Reaching Teenagers	WAH	Andy Peck & Martin Saunders
ep	Understanding Yourself, Understanding Others (MBTI® Basic)	WAH	Lynn & Andrew Penson
Sep	Bible in a Day	WAH	Andy Peck
ep	Help! I Want to Read the Bible (FREE EVENT)	WAH	Andy Peck & Lynette Brooks
Sep	Career Changes and Choices	WAH	Stephen & Rosalyn Derges
30 Sep	Women's Weekend: 'In His Presence'	WAH	Lynn Penson & Rosalyn Derges
Oct	Bible Discovery Weekend: 'David – the Man After God's Own Heart'	WAH	Philip Greenslade
ct	Insight into Depression	WAH	Chris Ledger
ct	Women's Autumn Day: 'Trust in the Lord with All Your Heart'	WAH	Lynn Penson
ct	Prayer Evening	WAH	Canon Andrew White tbc
ct	Developing Pastoral Care (Part 1)	WAH	Andy Peck, Philip Greenslade, Lynn Penson & team
ct	Small Group Leaders' Toolbox	Pilgrim Hall	Andy Peck
ct	Depression and Anxiety – Helping Teenagers with Hidden Problems	WAH	Chris Ledger
ct	Personality and Spirituality	WAH	Lynn & Andrew Penson

se also pray for students and tutors on our ongoing **BA in Counselling** programme at Waverley and our **ificate and Diploma of Christian Counselling** and **MA in Integrative Psychotherapy** held at London ol of Theology.

For further details and a full list of CWR's courses,
phone +44 (0)1252 784719, or visit the CWR website
at **www.cwr.org.uk**

Revealed – not discovered

FOR READING & MEDITATION – ROMANS 11:25-36

'Oh, the depth of the riches of the wisdom and knowledge of God! How unsearchable his judgments, and his paths beyond tracing out!' (v.33)

We are ready now to begin looking at some of the ways in which God works, but before we do so we pause in the light of today's text to ask ourselves this question: if God's ways are 'unsearchable and past finding out', why try to discover them?

The point this text makes is that it is impossible for the human mind *on its own* to search out and understand the designs of God. It is not saying we cannot understand them; it is saying that we cannot understand them by our own unaided reason. Therefore, God has graciously revealed something of His ways through Scripture, and one of the main purposes of the Bible is to help us become familiar with the ways, will, plans and purposes of God. So, without any further preamble, let's dig into Scripture and see what we can learn about our Father's ways.

FURTHER STUDY

John 6:5-13;
1 Cor. 2:6-16

1. How did Jesus sometimes relate to His disciples?

2. Why can we understand the things of God?

I have highlighted for our meditations over the next few weeks eight specific *ways of God*, and the first to come under consideration is this – *it is the way of God to train before He entrusts.* God will never place us in a position of great responsibility in His kingdom without first putting us through some spiritual training. The apostle Paul said: '... he considered me faithful, appointing me to his service' (I Tim. 1:2).

A.S. Way translates it thus: 'He tested me ... ere He entrusted me.' Believe me, if you want to do something great for God, you must be willing to be tried and proved. And the 'testing' is not so much that God might be convinced of your ability to perform, but that you yourself might become more refined and ready through the process.

Father, help me understand that I must not look upon Your training as an obstacle I have to overcome, but as an opportunity to be grasped. For I see that it is as I grapple that I grow. Amen.

He is looking still

FOR READING & MEDITATION - MARK 12:35-44

'Jesus sat down opposite the place where the offerings were put and watched the crowd putting their money into the temple treasury.' (v.41)

We said yesterday that everyone who seeks to do something great for God must be prepared to undergo spiritual training as preparation. What are some aspects of our training? I have discovered, both in my own life and in talking with others, that there are five or six major areas of training or preparation that God uses before He entrusts us with special responsibility in His kingdom.

One is our financial stewardship. Our text tells us that Jesus 'sat down opposite the treasury, and watched …' I believe He is watching still. I remember very clearly, in the early years of CWR, when just hundreds of pounds went through my hands, how the Lord spoke to me and said: 'I am watching how you handle this responsibility. Do it well and I will give you greater things to take care of for Me.' Later, as CWR grew, thousands of pounds went through my hands, and again the Lord came alongside me and said, in the tenderest way: 'I am still watching.'

I made mistakes, of course, but they were not major ones and were easily rectified. Now, along with my fellow directors, I am a trustee of a property of significant value.

One of the things I find saddest is to see a young man start out in the work of God with tremendous spiritual potential and then fail the money test. I know some Christians, and so I am sure do you, who looked as if they were going to set the world on fire, but because they couldn't handle money they fell by the way. It is a sobering thought, but Jesus still sits quietly by the treasury, carefully watching how we handle money, and the influence and effect it has on us.

FURTHER STUDY

Luke 18:18-25;
John 12:1-8

1. How did Jesus test if the ruler's spiritual desire was genuine?

2. What was Judas's first act of betrayal?

O God my Father, I see so clearly that money can be a ministry or it can be my master. Help me see that I am a steward not a proprietor, and that everything I have is part of a sacred trust - Your trust. Amen.

The time test

FOR READING & MEDITATION - COLOSSIANS 4:1-18
'... make the most of every opportunity.' (v.5)

We continue looking at some of the areas of our lives in which God works as He prepares us for special responsibility in His kingdom. Jesus sits alongside us, not only to look at how we use our treasure, but also at how we use our time. One of the greatest tests of discipleship is what we do with the minutes and hours that are entrusted to us day by day.

I am convinced that if I had not learned to become a good manager of my time, I would never have been able to continue writing issue after issue of *Every Day with Jesus*, which is now read by hundreds of thousands of people around the world. In the words of John Wesley, that master user of time: 'Never be unemployed and never be triflingly employed.'

FURTHER STUDY

Prov. 24:30-34;
Luke 10:38-42

1. What may be the result of wasted time?

2. How can we be too busy?

In photography, we are told that the quality of the picture depends, not only on what you put into it, but what you leave out. Likewise, our capacity to say 'No' determines our capacity to say 'Yes'. You have to say 'No' to lesser things in order to say 'Yes' to greater things. Life, it has been said, 'demands elimination as well as assimilation'. That is why the first qualification of a writer is – a wastepaper basket. Throw away things that do not contribute.

Can you pass the 'time' test? Do you carry on conversations, for example, long after they have run out of intelligence? Or waste hours daydreaming? Time is distilled opportunity – a sacred trust. Don't waste it, for in doing so you waste yourself. People often say to me: 'My problem is that I don't have enough time.' I have often responded: 'No, that's not your problem, your problem is that you do not use to the best advantage the time you have.'

My Father and my God, I want to be ready for whatever You have for me in the future. Help me make the most of every moment, so that when the great moments come I will be a prepared person. In Christ's name I ask it. Amen.

Be a finisher

FOR READING & MEDITATION - LUKE 12:35-48

'Who then is the faithful and wise manager, whom the master puts in charge of his servants ...?' (v.42)

Another area of our life which God uses to prepare us for special responsibility in His kingdom is persistence. Talk to any spiritual leader you know and I will guarantee that somewhere in their life you will find that God brought them to a time when they felt like giving up – but kept going nevertheless. The Church is filled with people who made good beginnings but bad endings. People start with good intentions but then, for various reasons, compromise on their original plans or become discouraged and give up.

One translation of the passage before us today says: 'Where is the trusty, thoughtful steward whom the lord and master will set over his establishment?' (Moffatt). Note the two words 'trusty' and 'thoughtful'. A 'trusty' servant will go through to the end, a 'thoughtful' servant will consider the best ways to achieve that end.

FURTHER STUDY

John 19:28-30;
2 Tim. 4:1-8

1. What could Jesus say?

2. What could Paul say?

Some time ago I watched a marathon race on television and saw a man come in hours behind the others. As he staggered towards the rope, weak and exhausted, the crowd applauded him more than they did the winner. And why? Because although he finished last – he *finished*. Everyone is impressed with a finisher. In 1 Corinthians chapter 16, the apostle Paul said: '... I'm staying right here ... A huge door of opportunity for good work has opened up here. (There is also mushrooming opposition.)' (vv.8–9, *The Message*). Many others might have said: 'I am quitting ... I have great opportunities here ... but there are too many things against me.' Determine, whatever God asks you to do, that you will stay with it – and finish it.

My Father, I know You want to use me. But I cannot be used unless I am trusty and thoughtful. Help me to be trusted to go through clear to the end with unwavering persistence. Amen.

The 'what is' test

FOR READING & MEDITATION – PHILIPPIANS 4:8-20

'... I have learned to be content whatever the circumstances.' (v.11)

We continue looking at some of the training which God puts His people through before He passes on to them greater responsibility in His kingdom. Today we look at what I am calling the 'what is' test. I am thinking here of those Christians who adopt the attitude: if I were anywhere but here, I would be all right. They dream of what they would do if they were not in their present circumstances. They are like birds in a cage, uselessly beating their wings because they cannot fly.

While it is true that it's important to have vision in our Christian experience and we need not stop desiring and longing for higher things, let's not allow the desire for 'what can be' to hinder us from living effectively in the 'what is'. The children of Israel lived on manna in the wilderness as they journeyed to the promised land. Imagine it – manna every day for 40 years! They got tired of it at times, but it sustained them right through the wilderness journey until they got to Canaan.

FURTHER STUDY

Psa. 55:1-8;
James 4:13-17

1. Describe the psalmist's attitude.

2. What type of people did Jesus address?

You and I may get tired of our present circumstances or situation, but we can learn to live with it until we get to our promised land. If I were to tell you the difficulties and problems that we encountered in remodelling Waverley Abbey House, you would have difficulty believing it. We might never have stayed with it if God had not taken us this way before and taught us the lesson of living with the 'what is' until we come to the moment of 'what will be'. If we can't get what we like, then we must like what we get. Learning that lesson gives a staying power that transforms everything.

Lord Jesus, You who lived on the manna of the silent years of obscurity in Nazareth – and lived on it gloriously – help me to live on the 'what is'. Then I shall really live. Amen.

The bread of life, with love ...

... from you, to Christians in need, both at home and overseas, who seek – like you – the sustenance of biblically-based guidance, teaching and resources.

In Galilee, Jesus told the crowd of over 4,000 to sit down,

'Then he took the seven loaves and the fish, and when he had given thanks, he broke them and gave them to the disciples, and they in turn to the people. They all ate and were satisfied' (Matt. 15:36-37).

With your help, the ministry of CWR can feed the faith of many.

Please fill in the 'Gift to CWR' section on the order form at the back of this publication, completing the Gift Aid declaration if appropriate.

Unfit for duty

FOR READING & MEDITATION - PSALM 141:1-10

'Set a guard over my mouth, O LORD; keep watch over the door of my lips.' (v.3)

Today we look at another area of training that God gives His servants before He entrusts them with special responsibility in His kingdom. This one has to do with that part of us which is comparatively small yet causes so much trouble – the tongue. Many a person has ruined a church fellowship as well as ship-wrecking their own spiritual future through unconsidered or unkind words. The expression of a thing deepens the impression of it, so a word uttered becomes a word made flesh – in us. In other words, some have said, 'We become what we express'.

FURTHER STUDY

James 3:1-18; Matt. 15:16-20

1. What was James' warning?

2. Why may our tongues fail the test?

I knew a man whose potential was so great that the college at which he was trained considered him to be a second Billy Graham. He took charge of a church and for a while things went well, until one of the church members offended his wife. Instead of taking the person to one side and discussing it on an individual basis, he chose to lash out at the whole church with words that were un-Christian and uncharacteristic. The church said: 'He is not the man we thought he was: nothing can justify such an outburst.' They lost confidence in him and today the man is in the spiritual doldrums – shut out of the ministry because he could not control his temper or his tongue.

Be assured of this – before God trusts anyone to greater responsibility and more accountable ministry, He is going to say what your doctor sometimes says when he examines you for some illness – 'Put out your tongue'. If it is a tongue that is stained by unrestraint and indiscipline, then He will have no other option than to regard you as unfit for duty – though not cast out.

O Father, help me understand that a word uttered becomes a word made flesh – in me. For my words will condemn me to be what they are; I become the incarnation of what I express. So save me from an undisciplined tongue. In Jesus' name. Amen.

'For Christ's sake'

FOR READING & MEDITATION - EPHESIANS 4:20-32

'Be kind and compassionate ... forgiving each other, just as in Christ
God forgave you.' (v.32)

This highly important issue of forgiveness is another
way in which God trains us before entrusting to our
care great spiritual responsibility. Some time ago, while
dining with a group of ministers, I was asked: what do
you think is the biggest single factor that causes spiritual
shipwreck in the lives of God's people? I hesitated, for many
things sprang to mind – jealousy, dishonesty, impurity,
prayerlessness, etc – but one thing stood out above all the
others: an inability to forgive.

Over the years, I have been privileged to listen to the
secret concerns of Christian leaders as they have
sought counselling for their problems and, time and
time again, I have heard them say this: 'Someone
has let me down badly and I have been deeply
hurt and offended. I find it almost impossible to
forgive.' I have heard this same story in many
parts of the world from men and women who
were on the threshold of a great ministry in the
kingdom – ministers, missionaries, evangelists,
elders and so on. I had to explain that unless they
were able to resolve the issue of forgiveness, they
would not go much further in the work of God.

Take my word for it, if you want to do anything
for God, come to terms with the fact before you start that
you are going to get hurt. People will disappoint you, tell
lies about you and vilify you – so prepare for it by learning
to forgive. And one area of learning to forgive is to do it
'for Christ's sake'. You may be unable to forgive on your
own, but with His help and by the breath of His Spirit, the
impossible becomes *Him*-possible.

**FURTHER
STUDY**

Matt. 18:21-35;
Heb. 12:14-15

1. What
did Jesus
teach about
forgiveness?

2. Why is
forgiveness so
important?

**O Father, You know the difficulties I have in forgiving those who
have hurt or offended me, so help me to be willing to be made
willing. Take my willingness and add to it Your power. With You, I
can do anything. Amen.**

For more on this issue, see the book *Insight into Forgiveness*, highlighted on page opposite 2 October.

FOR READING & MEDITATION - PROVERBS 3:11-26

'My son, do not despise the Lord's discipline ... because the Lord disciplines those he loves, as a father the son he delights in.' (vv.11-12)

The final area I would like us to look at is that of desires and wants. Many are ruled by desires they cannot control and so they hinder themselves in their spiritual journey. It has been said that 'the future of the world is in the hands of disciplined people'. I would go further and say that the future of the world is in the hands of those who know how to discipline themselves in the ways of the kingdom.

Desires are God-given areas of the personality and as such are right. Physical desires for things such as food, drink, sex, etc are natural desires, but when they are demanding and undisciplined they become a hindrance rather than a help to our daily living.

FURTHER STUDY

1 Cor. 9:24-27; Heb. 12:1-13

1. How did Paul handle his desires?

2. Why is discipline so important?

Take food, for example – some Christians are prone to what is known as 'comfort eating'; they find their comfort in food rather than in their heavenly Father.

Then there is the subject of drink – many are drawn to stimulants and alcohol. God knows it would not be good for us if under pressure we went to physical comfort to anaesthetise our pain instead of to God Himself – this is a dangerous path.

I am sure that everyone reading these lines will know of someone with a promising position in Christian work who has come to a sudden stop because they have let their sexual desire run away with them and have entered into an illicit and unhealthy relationship. As one leader put it: John the Baptist was not the only preacher to lose his head over a woman!

Heavenly Father, help me to harness all my desires and to drive them in Your purposes, for if I don't - they will drive me. I am either a servant or a master. Let nothing master me - except You. In Jesus' name. Amen.

When entering a tunnel

FOR READING & MEDITATION - PSALM 119:25-40

'Let me understand the teaching of your precepts;
then I will meditate on your wonders.' (v.27)

We turn now to consider another of the 'ways' of God –
those seemingly strange and unpredictable actions of
His which baffle human intelligence, yet have a wise and
benevolent purpose running through them. The next one on
which we focus is *the way in which God sometimes guides
us in a certain direction and then appears to abandon us,
leaving us struggling and confused in what appears to be
the most difficult and discouraging circumstances.*

Have you ever found yourself pressing forward with a
clear leading from God when, for no apparent reason, He
suddenly changes gear and puts everything into
reverse? Many Christians have gone through
this experience, and if you are there right now
– don't panic. God knows what He is doing; it's
one of His ways of moving us towards maturity
and bringing to pass an eternal and not just a
temporal purpose.

**FURTHER
STUDY**

Psa. 77:1-20;
119:9-16

1. What is the
nature of
God's ways?

This particular 'way' of God can be summed
up in this phrase – He reveals, reverses and then
restores. First God reveals His purpose, then after
a while He proceeds to reverse it so that it looks
on the surface of things as though He has either
abandoned His original intention or changed His
mind. Then, at His own appointed time, He brings the
original purpose to pass in His unmistakable manner.
Believe me, if we had not understood this principle during
the days when we were in the process of negotiating for
Waverley Abbey House, we would have been overcome
by a good deal of anxiety. All the great acts of God have
behind them this principle, and the more acquainted we
are with it, the more secure and confident we will be when
the train of divine guidance leads us into a dark tunnel.

2. What did
the psalmist
consider and
act upon?

**Gracious and loving heavenly Father, I see even more clearly
that a lot of my anxieties stem from my inability to know and
understand Your ways. Therefore I come before You once more
with the prayer: O Lord, teach me Your ways. Amen.**

Can God be too late?

FOR READING & MEDITATION – GENESIS 12:1-9

'I will make you into a great nation and I will bless you;
I will make your name great ...' (v.2)

We ended yesterday with the thought that all great acts of God have behind them this principle: He reveals, reverses, then restores. This is a biblical truth that I believe can be traced from Genesis through to Revelation. We see it clearly illustrated, for example, in the life of the patriarch Abraham. As our reading for today shows, God revealed to him that he would become the father of a great and mighty nation. Abraham was in no doubt that God had spoken to him, and by faith set out on a journey to an unknown destination.

FURTHER STUDY

Psa. 75:1-10;
Rom. 4:13-25;
Heb. 6:13-19

1. Who is in charge?

2. What characterises the attitude of Abraham?

Later, this revelation appeared to go into reverse when it became obvious that Sarah, his wife, was barren. Naturally, Abraham was confused. He reminded God that, despite the divine promise, he still had no child, whereupon God reaffirmed the fact that from Abraham would spring a nation that would be more in number than the stars in the heavens (Gen. 15:5).

Despite this repeated promise, however, Sarah passed the age of child-bearing so that, humanly speaking, it looked as though God had left things too late. His revealed purpose seemed to have gone so far in reverse that it could never be restored. But that is, it seems, precisely how God delights to do things. It is His way to let things go until they look as if there is no way they can be turned around, and then He steps in to ensure that His plans and purposes persist. Perhaps you are in this very situation at the moment – the situation of seeing something God has revealed to you go into reverse. If so, then don't be discouraged. Hold steady – this is one of Your Father's all-wise, albeit confusing, ways.

O Father, how can I ever be grateful enough to You for showing me through Scripture the wonder of Your ways. Burn deep within me the consciousness that all things proceed according to Your plan – even when they go into reverse. Amen.

FOR READING & MEDITATION - GENESIS 37:1-28

'... his brothers pulled Joseph up out of the cistern and sold him for twenty shekels of silver to the Ishmaelites ...' (v.28)

Yesterday we saw how the principle that God reveals, reverses and restores was illustrated in the life of the patriarch Abraham. Today we see that same principle illustrated in the life of Joseph. 'For colour and kaleidoscopic effect,' said Dr W.E. Sangster, 'the story of Joseph ranks with the *Arabian Nights* and is one of the most moving narratives in the whole of Scripture.'

Who could disagree? When Joseph was a young man, God revealed to him through a dream that he would play an important part in the plans and purposes of God. But not long after the revelation was given, it suddenly went into reverse when he was sold by his brothers to some slave traders on their way to Egypt and finished up as a slave in Potiphar's house. I wonder what Joseph thought to himself during those hard and difficult days as a slave in Egypt. Did he ponder on his dreams and question the reality of God's message to his heart? Whether he did or not we shall never know, but one thing is certain – the revelation that seemed to go significantly into reverse was, at God's appointed time, most wonderfully restored.

FURTHER STUDY

Gen. 50:15-26;
Psa. 105:17-24;
Heb. 11:22

1. What was Joseph's view of his troubles?

2. How did he view his own death?

Let me remind you of the events that brought him from being a prisoner to prime minister. Promoted, in the passing of time, to overseer in the prison, he became renowned for his ability to interpret dreams. Then, in that momentous hour when he solved the perplexities of Pharaoh's mind, he stepped in one mighty stride from being a prisoner with a few privileges to the Keeper of the Royal Seal with an authority second only to the throne.

Gracious and loving heavenly Father, as I see this divine principle so clearly illustrated in Your Word, help me to recognise it just as clearly when it is at work in my own life and circumstances. In Jesus' name. Amen.

God's way of preparation

FOR READING & MEDITATION - EXODUS 2:11-25

'Who made you ruler and judge over us? Are you thinking of killing
me as you killed the Egyptian?' (v.14)

Today we see the same principle at work in the life of another Old Testament patriarch – Moses. First God revealed His plan and purpose to him, then reversed it and finally restored it.

When Moses was a young man, he became deeply concerned for the plight of his Hebrew kinsmen who were in bondage to Pharaoh. Did God reveal to him at that time that he was to become the one who would lead His people from slavery to freedom? There is no verse of Scripture that says this, but I think it is safe to assume that rising within Moses was a sense of destiny and an awareness that he had been saved from death for a divine purpose.

FURTHER STUDY

Phil. 1:3-6;
Heb. 11:24-28

1. Why can we be confident in the face of reversal?

2. Why did Moses persevere?

Most Bible commentators feel that the verse which says: 'After Moses had grown up, he went out to where his own people were and watched them at their hard labour' (v.11) suggests that there was forming within Moses' mind the conviction that he was there for a divine purpose. Doubtless his mother would have told him of the promise which God had given to Abraham that one day the Hebrew nation would be brought into a land flowing with milk and honey, and would also have acquainted him with the ways in which God had supernaturally preserved the people of Israel.

So although we cannot say for certain that God revealed to Moses that he was to be the deliverer of His people, I believe myself that this conviction was forming in his mind. Assuming this to be so, then no sooner did the God-given idea arise than it went into reverse. Following the murder of the Egyptian, Moses was rejected by his kinsmen and forced to flee into the desert where he stayed for 40 years.

My Father and my God, I am grateful for this daily exposure to Your Word. Help me see that this truth which is confronting me is not a whim of Yours but a way. Reveal it to me even more clearly, dear Lord. Amen.

Endings and beginnings

FOR READING & MEDITATION - MATTHEW 26:57-75
'... and going inside he sat with the guards to see the end.'
(v.58, ESV)

Today we look at a New Testament example of how God reveals, reverses – and then restores. When Jesus was here on earth, He began His ministry by announcing the news that He was in the world to establish a kingdom – the kingdom of God. Listen to how Matthew puts it: 'From that time on Jesus began to preach, "Repent, for the kingdom of heaven is near"' (Matt. 4:17).

Throughout the three-and-a-half-year period of His public ministry, Jesus put before men the dazzling prospect of a kingdom in which He was the rightful King. Multitudes responded to that message and, at one stage, so successful were the circumstances surrounding the Son of God that some of His disciples began to argue about who should sit at His side in the coming kingdom. It seemed to them that Jesus was about to oust the empire of Rome and become the King of Israel.

At the end of His three-and-a-half-year period of ministry, however, the revelation of the coming kingdom suddenly went into reverse. The Saviour was brought before His captors and treated like a common criminal. Simon Peter thought, as our text for today suggests, that this was the end; the things that Jesus had said about the coming kingdom were nothing more than a dream. The revelation Jesus had given concerning the kingdom of God was seemingly at a point where it could never be restored. Whoever survived a crucifixion? But three days after Jesus' death on the cross, God miraculously raised Him from the dead and restored to the dispirited Peter, as well as the rest of the disciples, the truth that had first captured their hearts.

FURTHER STUDY

2 Kings 6:24-7:20

1. Contrast the attitudes of the king and Elisha.

2. Why should we never give up hope?

O Father, help me understand that when the revelation You have given me goes into reverse, it is not the beginning of the end, but the end of the beginning. Thank You, dear Father. Amen.

It's time to celebrate

FOR READING & MEDITATION - HABAKKUK 2:1-4

'For the revelation awaits an appointed time ... Though it linger, wait for it; it will certainly come ... (v.3)

Having explored over the past few days several examples of how when God reveals something, the next thing He does is to change gear and put things in reverse, we now ask ourselves this question: does God follow this same pattern with all His revelations?

No, not all of God's leadings follow this pattern – but the major ones, I believe, always do. Read the biographies of great Christian leaders or the histories of famous Christian movements and organisations and you will invariably find that after God revealed His plans and purposes to them, the next thing He did was to put things into reverse. Then, at an appropriate moment and in His own good time, He restored the original revelation in a miraculous and supernatural manner.

FURTHER STUDY

Acts 2:22-36;
7:55-8:8

1. What is our ultimate basis of confidence and celebration?

2. What was the result of persecution?

I said a few days ago that if we had not understood this divine principle when we set out to purchase Waverley Abbey House, we would have experienced a good deal of anxiety. The moment Trevor Partridge and I saw Waverley Abbey House, we felt a witness of the Spirit that our search for a property in which to house a Christian teaching and training centre was over. God revealed to us that this was to be the place. But, a few weeks later, we were told that it was in the process of being sold to someone else and there was no point in pursuing the matter further. The clearly revealed plans of God were now in reverse. We rested in the confidence, however, of knowing that though the vision God had revealed might go into reverse, it would inevitably be restored. The ministry of Waverley Abbey House is a testimony to that restoration.

O Father, I see even more clearly that the more I understand Your way, the more I will be able to find my own way when I am caught up in situations that don't seem to make sense. So give me my lessons and help me to learn. Amen.

Reasons for reversals

FOR READING & MEDITATION – ZECHARIAH 4:1-10

'"Not by might nor by power, but by my Spirit,"
says the LORD Almighty.' (v.6)

It is now time to ask the question: why does God adopt
these seemingly mysterious methods of working to
reveal something to us and then put things in reverse? It
is not because He likes to tease us or play mind games.
No – He does it this way because I believe when God
reveals something to us, He knows that at the moment
of some fresh unfolding of His will, we have within us a
combination of godly concerns and human perspectives.
We are eager, alert and full of natural enthusiasm. He also
knows that our natural enthusiasm is the thing that helps
us get going to do His will; but a moment has to
come when our natural enthusiasm is overlaid by
divine perspectives.

How does God achieve this? He allows us to go
ahead in the strength of our own eagerness and
then, at the appropriate moment, He changes gear
and puts things into reverse. When we come to
this point, we realise that if the revelation that
God has given us is to be realised, then it will not
be because of our strength and abilities – but His.

When we learn that lesson, then God intervenes
to restore His purposes – often in a miraculous
and surprising way. Note the word 'miraculous'.
The fact that things are restored miraculously is then a
constant reminder that God will always have the biggest
part in a project. In that way, no onlooker can be in doubt as
to who is responsible for the success – everyone recognises
it to be God.

If things are in reverse in your life at the moment, then
rest assured – God knows what He is doing. The vision will
be restored. It is His way.

FURTHER STUDY

Psa. 20:1-9;
1 Cor. 2:1-5

1. Contrast where the psalmist and others put their trust.

2. What was Paul's concern?

O Father, the way You reveal and restore is so exciting – it's the
middle bit I don't like. Yet I see I have to go through it if Your
purposes are to be worked out in me. Help me to remember this
the next time things go into reverse. Amen.

Changing perspective

FOR READING & MEDITATION - COLOSSIANS 1:1-14

'... asking God to fill you with the knowledge of his will through all spiritual wisdom and understanding.' (v.9)

We continue looking at some of our heavenly Father's ways – ways which, from a human perspective, seem strange and confusing but, when fully understood, are seen to contain the most profound purposes and the most astonishing wisdom.

Another of His ways we will look at is *the way He takes us by the hand and places us in situations where everything appears to go wrong.* You would think that if God loved us as much as He says He does, He would lead us, not into confusing and unclear situations, but away from them. And, as we know, difficulties have an uncanny way of coming together. For a while, everything in life is going well. Then suddenly, for no apparent reason, the skies are filled with thick and threatening clouds. A family member is struck down with illness, business difficulties seem to shut one in on every side, and the whole world seems to tumble about one's ears.

At such times we cry out: why is God allowing this to happen to me? How can God say He loves me when He fails to answer my prayers and deliver me from such dark and difficult experiences? Ah, my friend, hold steady – there is a reason. It may appear on the surface of things that God has lost control – but nothing could be further from the truth. He never loses control of anything. If you could but penetrate the depths of the divine heart, you would see a purpose being worked out that would more than compensate for your feelings of uncertainty and doubt. We so often see things from our point of view – He sees things from His. Peace comes when you can change your perspective to His.

FURTHER STUDY

Gen. 45:1-11; Ezek. 16:3-14

1. How was God's perspective different to Joseph's brothers?

2. Contrast the perspectives of God and people.

Gracious Master, I would walk amid adversity with my head held high. But I cannot do this unless I bow at Your feet and learn Your ways. Help me see everything that happens to me from Your point of view. In Jesus' name. Amen.

'God's latchstring'

FOR READING & MEDITATION - 2 CORINTHIANS 9:6-15

'And God is able to make all grace abound to you ...' (v.8)

We continue considering the question: why does God sometimes lead us into situations where everything seems to go wrong? One answer to that question is this – it is God's way to focus more on the development of our characters than on the development of our happiness.

If you do not understand this – or are not willing to understand it – then you will find the hard and confusing situations in your life become even harder. Always remember this – the end of life is not happiness, but growth in character and spiritual maturity. And how can God develop our growth in character? There is one way – situations that are hard enough for us to sharpen our souls upon.

When I was an engineering student in my teens, I was taught that to get a sharp cutting edge on a machine tool, I needed to sharpen it against something that was much harder – an emery stone. Sometimes an emery stone would be faulty and too soft – hence ineffective. In pursuing the goal of growth in character, we may find ourselves in situations which not only make growth possible, but stimulate it.

Here's something else you need to get hold of – whenever you find yourself in a situation which looks as if it is too difficult to cope with, you can depend on it that all the resources you need to help you stand up to the pressure have already been provided through the foresight of a loving God. And where do we find these resources? In Jesus Christ. As one little boy put it: 'Jesus is God's latchstring hung so low that anybody can reach it.'

FURTHER STUDY

Acts 20:32-35;
Heb. 4:14-16

1. What is God's grace able to do for us?

2. How can we avail ourselves of God's grace?

O Father, what a thought to begin a day – You have provided everything for my growth in character. When in difficult situations You make available to me the grace I need to make them make me. I am so grateful. Amen.

From this place ...

This September, CWR celebrates 25 years of ministry at Waverley Abbey House, Surrey, England. In 1987, CWR's founders and directors – Selwyn Hughes, Trevor Partridge and David Rivett – opened the doors of the refurbished Georgian building, and a bold new vision began to unfold: to equip men and women of conviction to build the Body of Christ and change their communities for good; to impact the Church, the nation and the world.

That first year included: a prayer retreat; teaching on many aspects of Christian counselling, biblical principles in medicine, law, business management, education and social work; biblical studies; and marriage enrichment. From the beginning came a balance of intense study and training, as well as a focus on relational issues, spiritual growth and discipleship. All this, as well as the continuance and development of CWR's publishing programme.

By God's grace, and with the support of CWR's Partners, many elements of the original vision have been achieved. Around 6,000 visitors and students are impacted each year, and millions are reached through Bible-reading resources, with the help of national distributors in 22 nations and translations in 48 languages. The ripple effect from Waverley Abbey House is both humbling and in the truest sense, awesome.

And it seems, in this anniversary year, no coincidence that another milestone has been reached. Growing pressure on space to accommodate our ever-increasing delegate numbers was alleviated when God opened a door for CWR to purchase Pilgrim Hall, a conference centre in East Sussex. This provided the facilities required to continue towards the goal of establishing a Christian college of education.

In its twenty-fifth year, Waverley Abbey House is set to become the pivotal hub for some exciting developments. With expectant hearts we thank God for the work He has begun here, and trust Him for the new chapters of *His* ministry. We thank you also for your continued interest and support, and ask for your prayers as we move forward.

Perhaps, to mark this significant year, you would like to become a CWR Partner. For more information, contact our Partnership Coordinator, Robin Pickford, on 01252 784707 or visit **www.cwr.org.uk/partners**

University training

FOR READING & MEDITATION - JAMES 1:1-12

'Consider it pure joy, my brothers, whenever you face trials
of many kinds ...' (v.2)

Regular readers of *Every Day with Jesus* will be aware that I often return to this verse. If the chief goal which God has for us is not the development of our happiness but the development of our character, then it is obvious that He has to place us in situations where our characters can be perfected. And these situations must be sufficiently hard to sharpen our souls upon.

We live in a beautiful world, but a world that has been deeply damaged by sin. In many ways it is a hard world – one that is beset with earthquakes, tsunamis, tornadoes, volcanoes, deadly viruses, snakes, weeds and other things that plague mankind. Those who see only the problems say to themselves: God cannot be a loving and perfect God, for if He were He would never have allowed His world to fall into such a state.

Others, however, take a different view. They see the hard side of the universe as an emery stone on which to sharpen their understanding. Instead of bemoaning the fact that deadly viruses exist, they set about the task of researching ways of combating them. When earthquakes come, they give themselves to finding ways of constructing buildings that can withstand them. Where they find weeds, they seek ways of getting rid of them. And what happens to such people? As they seek to improve the world around them, they succeed also in improving themselves.

It is the same in the Christian life. If we don't grow in character, it isn't because God has failed to set the stage for our growth; it is because we fail to sharpen our souls on the hard situations in which He places us. After all, the best university is the University of Adversity.

FURTHER STUDY

2 Cor. 1:3-11;
4:5-18

1. What did Paul learn in the University of Adversity?

2. Where was his focus?

O Father, help me to take every situation and use it to sharpen my soul. It is Your way to put character before happiness – help me to make it my way too. In Jesus' name I ask it. Amen.

What if He left us alone?

FOR READING & MEDITATION - ROMANS 8:26-39

'For those God foreknew he also predestined to be conformed
to the likeness of his Son ...' (v.29)

Suppose God left us alone and we never found ourselves
in perplexing and difficult situations – what would
happen to us? Without something hard on which to
sharpen our souls, we would become dull and lacking in
initiative. We talked yesterday of those who respond to
the challenge of a world in which there are earthquakes,
tsunamis, deadly viruses and so on by seeking out ways to
overcome the problems these things produce. But someone
says: 'This may be true, but dealing with a hard universe is
one thing – dealing with hard people is another.'

Well, what about this environment of people?
What do we do when we find ourselves among
difficult and irritating people? I am persuaded
that this, too, can be part of God's purpose to
develop character within us. I know many who
have grown to be better persons as a direct result
of being surrounded by difficult and irritating
people. If God has put you among people who try
your patience, then decide that you will make this
not a groaning point, but a growing point.

I knew a woman in South Wales who was
married to an extremely difficult man. He drank
far too much, criticised her, shouted at her and did
everything he could to make her life miserable. She found
herself in an awful situation, but she learned what she
could and was able to say: 'My circumstances are helping
me grow more like Jesus every day.' I was staggered both
by her words and by her radiant, integrated personality.
Was this development of her character 'in spite of' her
environment? No, it was because of it. She made her
environment make her.

**FURTHER
STUDY**

2 Cor. 6:1-10;
1 Pet. 4:12-19

1. How did Paul
respond to
suffering?

2. What should
be our response
to personal
suffering?

**My Father and my God, help me see that nothing can be greater
than the development of character. And no character can be
greater than the character of Jesus. Teach me how to make my
circumstances make me more and more like Him. Amen.**

Rough refining

FOR READING & MEDITATION - 1 PETER 1:1-13

'These have come so that your faith ... may be proved genuine and may result in praise, glory and honour ...' (v.7)

We are seeing that even a hostile environment can be used by God to develop and deepen our character. Just as an aircraft, when taking off, rises against the wind, so we can rise against the adverse winds of difficult situations to become more and more like Jesus. This is just another of God's ways of building character in us, and if we do not understand this principle, we may end up bitter rather than better.

Can character be developed in serene and peaceful circumstances? The story is told of a man who found himself in a position where every wish was immediately fulfilled and where every difficulty that confronted him was immediately resolved. He wanted a house – and there it was with servants at the door. He wanted a Rolls Royce and one appeared before him – complete with a uniformed chauffeur. He felt quite elated at the prospect of being able to have anything he wished for, but as time went on and more and more of his wishes were granted, the whole thing began to irritate him. He said to an attendant: 'I want to get out of this situation as fast as I can. It is getting me down. I long to achieve something, to create something. I would rather be in hell than this.' The attendant answered: 'Where do you think you are?'

The world in which we live contains, it seems, an endless variety of adversities such as disease, earthquakes and so on, but awaiting our discovery are remedies for every one of them. In the midst of every difficulty and problem, there are always surprises in store for those who know where to look.

FURTHER STUDY

Psa. 66:8-20;
Isa. 43:1-7

1. How did the psalmist fulfil the vows he made when in trouble?

2. What consolation do we have in fiery trials?

O Father, when next I find myself in a situation where everything seems to be going wrong, I know exactly where I am going to look – I am going to look to You. Help me to turn everything to the deepening of my character. Amen.

Don't sink – soar!

FOR READING & MEDITATION – ISAIAH 40:21-31

'... but those who hope in the LORD will ... soar on wings like eagles ...'
(v.31)

I have often wondered why it is that two Christians can go through the exact same set of difficult circumstances and yet react quite differently. One takes the difficult circumstances and sharpens his soul on them, thereby making himself more spiritually alert and responsive, while the other allows them to bring him down into defeat and discouragement.

Many reasons, of course, could be argued, but the biggest single reason (in my opinion) is that one knows and understands the way God works, while the other does not. *Soaring above the Storm*, a previous *Every Day with Jesus*, explored in detail the fact that if an eagle's wings are set at a downward tilt when a storm strikes, it will be dashed to the ground, but if its wings are tilted upward, it will rise, making the storm bear it up beyond its fury. The tilt of the wings decides life or death.

Knowing and understanding what God is about when we are placed in dark and difficult circumstances enables us to tilt our wings in the right direction. When things are falling apart and nothing seems to be going right, we tilt our wings heavenward and say: 'Lord, I know that You are working all things for my good, and through this situation You are going to make me more like Jesus than I have ever been before. Therefore I will rise with You to see the whole thing from Your point of view.' If we can do this, then instead of being dashed to the ground in bitterness and confusion, we will soar into the heavens with Christ and come out into quiet peace and greater usefulness.

FURTHER STUDY

Acts 16:16-34

1. How did Paul and Silas rise above their situation?

2. What was the result?

O God, more than ever I see that the right attitude results in the right altitude. When I am placed in trying circumstances, show me how to get the tilt of my wings right. I don't want to sink, I want to soar. Help me, Father. Amen.

God's sowing - our harvest

FOR READING & MEDITATION - JOB 23:1-12
'... when he has tested me, I shall come forth as gold.' (v.10)

We spend one more day meditating on the fact that one of God's ways is sometimes to lead us into situations where everything seems to go wrong. He does this, as we have said, because He knows that this is one of the ways in which He can bring about the development of our character – so we can move into His plans and purposes.

Again I have to say that if God had not taught us this lesson prior to our purchase and remodelling of Waverley Abbey House, then our wings would have had a downward tilt and we would have crashed in the dust of defeat and discouragement. At one stage it seemed that everything that could go wrong, did go wrong. It would have been impossible for anyone, even the most experienced architect or builder, to have predicted at the start of the remodelling process the number of problems that could arise – but arise they did. On one occasion things looked very dark and difficult, but we reminded ourselves that God had placed us in this situation and though things were going drastically wrong, He was pursuing His purposes nevertheless.

FURTHER STUDY

Psa. 139:13-24;
Zech. 13:9

1. What was the psalmist's desire?

2. What was the result of bringing people into the fire?

Many times we encouraged one another with these and similar words, and those especially who were involved in the decision-making and bore final responsibility all testify to the fact that God refined our natures, sensitised our souls and deepened our characters in the process. Edward Markham says that 'troubles and trials stretch our hearts for joy'. They do, and more – they stretch our hearts for new achievements, new usefulness and deeper character. Troubles plough the field for God's sowing, and our harvest – the harvest of character.

O Father, I am so thankful that Your ways are not the ways of a tyrant or dictator who just likes to have his own way - they are the ways of a Deity who has our highest good at heart. I am so thankful. Amen.

'Slow growth'

FOR READING & MEDITATION - EXODUS 23:20-33

'Little by little I will drive them out from before you,
until you have increased ...' (v.30)

We continue meditating on our heavenly Father's wondrous ways. The one we consider now is a characteristic of God which, if not learned and understood, can lead to a good deal of frustration and confusion.

The thought I want to bring before you can best be seen by comparing two different passages of Scripture. In our text for today, we read that God tells the children of Israel that when the time comes for them to enter the promised land, they will overcome their enemies - '*little by little*'. Over in Deuteronomy 9:3, however, He says: 'You shall drive them out and destroy them *quickly*'. One passage says the enemies would be overcome slowly, the other says it would happen quickly – which is it to be? Is this a divine contradiction? No, for further exploration or reading shows that *some* enemies would be overcome slowly, taking years, while *others* would fall quickly and be conquered in a day.

These two apparently opposing texts reveal another intriguing aspect of God's ways – *He purposes that we overcome some problems quickly, while others take a considerable length of time.* Dr Lawrence Crabb, to whom I am indebted for this insight, calls it 'the principle of slow growth'. The children of Israel entering the promised land is, as you may be aware, a picture of the Christian life. Although we move into all that God has promised, we still find that there are problems. And some of these problems are overcome slowly, while others are overcome quickly. Knowing part of God's purpose in this can once again make all the difference between perplexity and peace.

FURTHER STUDY

1 Pet. 2:1-2;
Heb. 5:11-6:3;
Gal. 4:19

1. To what does the Bible compare new Christians?

2. What was Paul's desire?

O Father, I am thankful that quietly, day by day, You are introducing me to thoughts and insights from Your Word that help me to understand You better. Lead on, dear Father - I am following. Amen.

'Instant solutions'

FOR READING & MEDITATION – 2 PETER 3:1-18

'But grow in the grace and knowledge of our Lord and Saviour Jesus Christ.' (v.18)

We ended yesterday with the thought that some of our problems are overcome quickly, while others seem to take a considerable length of time to resolve. Have you discovered this in your own life and experience? Do you find yourself struggling day after day with some problems, yet overcoming others with surprising ease? This is because there is a divine principle at work in your life; our heavenly Father is doing with you what He did with the children of Israel – bringing you through some problems quickly, while ensuring that others take a longer time.

FURTHER STUDY

2 Thess. 1:1-4;
James 5:7-8;
2 Pet. 1:3-11

1. What was noticeable about the Thessalonians?

2. How can we add to our faith?

I know that to some, this thought suggests defeatism. They will say: 'God's power is great enough to enable us to overcome all our problems quickly, and to suggest otherwise is a denial of His might. When we are filled with the Spirit, all our problems can be dealt with quickly.' I understand that view and, at one time, would have subscribed to it myself, but years of studying Scripture, as well as personal involvement in the lives and circumstances of thousands of people, have convinced me that, for good reasons, some problems are not overcome quickly – they are only overcome through 'slow growth'.

I am afraid that one of the errors plaguing the Church is that of preaching a gospel of 'instant solutions'. I have heard it said: 'Come to Christ and all your problems will be instantly resolved.' It is not true. It is true to say that when we come to Christ, we have the potential for overcoming all our problems, but it is not true to say that they can all be *instantly* resolved. Some are resolved quickly, others slowly. Don't let anyone persuade you otherwise.

Gracious and loving heavenly Father, save me from the peril of expecting either too little or too much. Help me to gain a balanced and truly biblical view of this issue. In Jesus' name I pray. Amen.

Giant-sized problems

FOR READING & MEDITATION - JOSHUA 11:1-20

'Joshua waged war against all these kings for a long time.' (v.18)

We continue meditating on the thought that some problems in our lives are overcome quickly, while others take much longer to resolve. How can we differentiate between the two? One answer can be found by once again comparing two separate passages of Scripture – Joshua 11 and Joshua 15.

Joshua was chosen by God to be Moses' successor and was given the task of leading the children of Israel into the promised land. In Joshua 11, we read of the exploits of Joshua and his armies after they had crossed over the Jordan, and verse 18 points out something very significant: 'Joshua waged war against all these kings for a long time.' Note the phrase – 'a long time'. Isn't this exactly what God had predicted? Had He not said that some enemies would take a long time to overcome and would be driven out 'little by little'?

However, in Joshua 15:14 are the exploits of Caleb, another great military strategist who appears to have gained a quick victory over the three sons of Anak – Sheshai, Ahiman and Talmai. We ask ourselves: who were these sons of Anak and what significance do they have in God's Word? You may remember that ten of the twelve spies who went into Canaan to evaluate the situation came back with a report that it contained 'men of great stature ... giants' (Num. 13:32–33, AV) – among whom were the three sons of Anak. It was these giants, who struck terror into the hearts of the ten spies and gave rise to their great unbelief. How fascinating that the problem which caused them to fear entering into the land yielded to a quick solution, while what they saw as a lesser problem took much longer to overcome.

FURTHER STUDY

Num. 13:26-33;
Josh. 14:6-15;
15:13-14

1. How did the spies view themselves?

2. How did Caleb view himself?

O Father, how can I thank You enough for placing within Your Word everything I need for effective Christian living. Help me to search the Scriptures daily so that I might know more of You and Your wondrous ways. Amen.

Little and large

FOR READING & MEDITATION - 1 CORINTHIANS 10:1-13

'These things happened to them as examples and were written down as warnings for us ...' (v.11)

We ended yesterday by saying that when the spies who were sent out to reconnoitre the land of Canaan saw 'the giants, the sons of Anak', they were overcome with fear. And when this fear gave rise to unbelief, it led to the children of Israel having to forfeit entering the land for a whole generation. It is also worth noting that Caleb and Joshua, the two who did not fear the giants, were the only ones of their generation to enter the promised land, and were used by God to overcome Israel's enemies.

FURTHER STUDY

Acts 10:9-15, 23-29;
Gal. 2:11-16

1. What did Peter battle for years?

2. Was Paul right to oppose him face to face?

We continue, however, to the thought that the big problems facing Israel's entrance into the promised land were overcome quickly, while the smaller or lesser ones took a considerable time to resolve. Is there a principle here that we can bring over into everyday Christian living? I believe there is. In fact, I would be surprised if you have not already observed this principle at work in your own life and experience. Have you found yourself wrestling for some time, perhaps even years, with something that is relatively small, while experiencing dramatic victories over the 'giant' problems that stand in your way?

As I look back on my early experience as a Christian, I can remember sometimes overcoming the big problems with amazing ease, yet struggling for years with things I considered to be much less demanding or threatening. Looking at it from a human perspective, one would think it ought to be the other way round – the smaller problems should be overcome quickly, while the bigger ones should take much longer. But it is not so for good reasons – it is not God's way.

O Father, I see that what seems right to me may seem all wrong to You. If I am to succeed as a Christian, then it is imperative that I look at things from Your point of view. Help me, Father. Amen.

Giant-sized victories

FOR READING & MEDITATION - 1 SAMUEL 17:32-51

'Your servant has killed both the lion and the bear; this uncircumcised Philistine will be like one of them ...' (v.36)

In the interests of clarity, we must pause for a few moments to gather up the threads of what we have been saying over the past few days. Our thoughts have focused around the fact that some problems we meet in life seem to be resolved quickly, while others take more time. And the type of problems that yield to quick resolutions are not, as we would expect, the small and simple ones, but the ones which are big and threatening.

We must now add one more thought to what we have been saying – a thought without which we would not be able to gain a clear perspective on this issue we are exploring or come to sound conclusions, and that is: quick and sudden victories come only after we have wrestled for some time with smaller and lesser issues. In other words, we need to learn to deal with the smaller issues before we can experience sudden resolution in the bigger ones.

Take, for example, David's victory over Goliath. How long did it take David to defeat the giant? A year? A month? A week? A day? No – it was all over in a moment. David put a stone in his sling, whirled it around his head, let it go and, within seconds, Goliath fell to the ground – dead. Notice, however, what our passage for today points out – David knew what it was to experience success in the day-to-day issues before taking on the giant that threatened Israel's physical and spiritual wellbeing (vv.32–37). Over the years, David had built up his experience and trust in dealing with the problems that came to him in his role as a shepherd, and so, when it came to facing the greater challenge of Goliath, he was ready for a quick and sudden triumph.

FURTHER STUDY

2 Sam. 21:15-22:7;
1 Chron. 20:4-8

1. How many giants did David and his men have to overcome?

2. How did David feel as a result of these battles?

O Father, help me to come to grips with the smaller issues of my life, so that when I am confronted with the giant-sized problems, I will be prepared and ready. I ask this in Jesus' name. Amen.

Supporting the depressed

FOR READING & MEDITATION - EPHESIANS 4:20-32

'Be kind to one another, tenderhearted,
forgiving one another ...' (v.32, ESV)

We continue meditating on the thought that the big problems of life are resolved more quickly and easily when we have had some experience of wrestling with the smaller, more day-to-day issues. I have often seen this principle at work in the lives of those who, for one reason or another, have been caught up in depression.

What can we say to someone who is depressed? 'In Jesus' name, claim the victory over your depression and command it to leave'? Or, 'Put on a happy smile and go out to meet the world'? Such statements, generally speaking, are not helpful. They may have a positive effect on some people, but mostly they cause hurt and the person may withdraw deeper into depression. A better way is to encourage them to come to grips with the smaller issues of life and experience resolution in them before moving on to bigger challenges.

A large percentage of Christians are depressed at one time or another. Rather than trying to find a 'quick fix', help those you are supporting to take small and steady steps forward. Many find it difficult to spend time praying and reading the Bible. Suggest they settle for a few minutes. If they don't feel like meeting or talking to many people in a day, then they could determine to talk to just one. If they don't feel like going for a long walk, then they could just go to the end of the street. By taking small steps in the day-to-day things, confidence is built up and they are then ready to face the bigger and greater challenges. And never say to a depressed person, 'Snap out of it.' That's about as helpful as telling a man to lift himself up by tugging at his shoelaces.

FURTHER STUDY

Judges 16:18-30;
Rom. 12:9-15

1. How long did it take for Samson's strength to return?

2. How should we respond to those who are depressed?

Gracious and loving heavenly Father, teach me to be a considerate and caring person. Help me to be more sensitive to those who are hurting, for perhaps today I might meet someone who needs my love and care. Amen.

For more on this issue, see *Insight into Depression*, highlighted on opposite page.

Insight into
Life's Big Issues

Throughout the year at Waverley Abbey House, 'Insight Days' are taught by experienced tutors on key current issues faced by individuals and families. Aimed at informing both sufferers and those seeking to care for or help others, topics include: addiction; anger; assertiveness; bereavement; dementia; eating disorders; perfectionism; self-esteem; sexual abuse; and stress, amongst others.

For full details/to book, visit www.cwr.org.uk or call +44 (0)1252 784719

An accompanying series of books is available, *The Waverley Abbey Insight Series*, and the following two books relate especially to topics covered in this issue:

INSIGHT INTO DEPRESSION
Chris Ledger and Wendy Bray
Recognise the symptoms of depression and debunk the myths about it. Gain a holistic and God-centred approach to recovery.
ISBN: 978-1-85345-538-4 **£8.99**

INSIGHT INTO FORGIVENESS
Ron Kallmier and Sheila Jacobs
Discover through real-life case studies, biblical examples and personal insights on how to live in freedom from the past.
ISBN: 978-1-85345-491-2 **£8.99**

Why we struggle

FOR READING & MEDITATION - PROVERBS 16:1-20
'Pride goes before destruction ...' (v.18)

We spend one more day meditating on the principle of 'slow growth'. We ask ourselves: what possible reason could God have had in planning for the Israelites to drive out some enemies slowly and others quickly? Part of the answer is found in a Scripture passage which we have already touched on – Exodus 23:29–30: 'I will not drive them out from before you in one year, lest the land become desolate for lack of attention and the wild beasts multiply against you. Little by little I will drive them out ... until you have increased and are numerous enough to take possession of the land' (Amp. Bible).

FURTHER STUDY

1 Pet. 5:5-11;
Rev. 3:14-22

1. Contrast God's response to the proud and the humble.

2. What was the problem of the Laodiceans?

If God had cleared the promised land of all its inhabitants prior to Israel taking possession, the task of managing it would have been too much for them. He therefore used the existing occupants to advance the purposes He had for His own people. Once we understand this principle – that God never acts arbitrarily but always purposefully – then we have the biggest single key to understanding His ways.

Had Israel taken possession of the land of Canaan without a struggle, they would most likely have become proud, independent and self-reliant. God saw to it that they had enough resistance to keep them dependent upon Him. They advanced slowly, but in a way that worked to their best advantage. Keep this in mind when you question why you still struggle with issues that you had hoped by now to have put behind you. (God would rather have you panting than proud.) Whilst you struggle over the smaller issues now, your spiritual muscles are being built up, and though you do not know it, you are being prepared and made ready for what lies ahead.

Father, I see that when I do not understand Your ways, I can so easily live against them - and get hurt. Once again I come to You with this simple but sincere prayer: Teach me Your ways, dear Lord. In Jesus' name. Amen.

Why? Why? Why?

THURS
4 OCT

FOR READING & MEDITATION - LUKE 11:1-13

'... how much more will your Father in heaven give the Holy Spirit to those who ask him!' (v.13)

We move on to look at yet another of our heavenly Father's ways – one which, in my experience, has caused many of God's children a good deal of bewilderment and consternation. I refer to *the way our heavenly Father has of appearing to withhold from us the very things He encourages us to pray for* – things which we know for sure are within the scope and compass of His perfect will. Sometimes it looks as if, with one hand, God encourages us to ask Him for spiritual blessings, and with the other, He withholds them from us.

This used to constantly puzzle me greatly when I first came into the Christian life. I remember hearing some of my Christian friends say such things as this: 'I prayed for an increase of spiritual power in my life and within days, I entered into a new awareness of God.' But then I would hear others say: 'I have prayed for that too, and to date, nothing seems to have happened.' I used to ask myself: 'Why is it that some Christians seem to get their prayers answered and others do not?' After thinking this through for a while, I came to the conclusion that perhaps it was because God had favourites, and that He liked some people better than others.

I held this erroneous belief for a long time until, one day, God opened up to me the passage that is before us today, and in it I discovered a principle which we shall look at in detail over the next few days. Just now, however, let me place this thought before you as a spiritual taster – when God appears to withhold a blessing from us, it is never because He is not ready to give but because we are not ready to receive.

FURTHER STUDY

Mark 14:32-35;
James 1:5-7

1. Why did God not grant Jesus' request?

2. How does doubt affect our prayers?

Gracious God and Father, help me come to a clearer understanding than ever before that You are a God who is not just willing to give, but eager to give. Help me to be as eager to receive. In Jesus' name. Amen.

What God delights to do

FOR READING & MEDITATION - PSALM 147:1-20

'... the LORD delights in those who fear him, who put their hope in his unfailing love.' (v.11)

We are asking ourselves why it is that God sometimes withholds from us the very things He encourages us to pray for – things which, beyond any doubt, are within the scope and compass of His will. In order to understand the divine intention behind this strange and mysterious 'way' of God, first we need to ask ourselves another and more basic question: does God really *delight* to give good things to His children? Is He really *eager* to give, or does He hand out His blessings dutifully, but with indifference?

It is very important that we have a clear understanding of the magnanimity and large-heartedness that exists in God, for any doubt about this can sabotage our whole approach to prayer. You see, if you are not absolutely sure that God is eager and willing to provide, you may not be able to approach Him with absolute confidence and this, in turn, will affect your feelings about Him, your spiritual expectancy and your ability to receive.

Let me illustrate – a farmer whose tractor had broken down decided to ask a neighbouring farmer if he could borrow his. As he set out across the fields, however, he began to have doubts about his neighbour's willingness to be of help, and the more he doubted, the more inclined he became to turn back. Before he knew where he was, however, he had reached the farmhouse, and upon catching sight of his neighbour, he blurted out: 'I have come to tell you that you can keep your rusty old tractor.' I say again – if you have doubts about the eagerness of God to provide, then you will not be in the right state of mind either to ask or to receive.

FURTHER STUDY

2 Sam. 7:1-22;
John 16:23-27

1. What surprised David?

2. What is the promise of Jesus?

O Father, help me at this point, for I see that if I take a wrong step here, I will take a wrong step everywhere. Burn deep into me the consciousness that You don't just give - You love to give. I am so thankful. Amen.

FOR READING & MEDITATION - LUKE 12:22-34

'Do not be afraid, little flock, for your Father has been pleased
to give you the kingdom.' (v.32)

We ended yesterday with the thought that any doubt
we may have concerning God's desire to provide will
greatly affect our desire to ask – and in consequence, our
readiness and willingness to receive. I believe myself that
Jesus must have had this thought very much in mind when
He told the story we read the other day, in Luke chapter II, of
the man who came at midnight to ask his friend for bread.

Did you notice how Jesus preceded that story by giving
His disciples a framework for prayer? We refer to it as
'The Lord's Prayer', but notice how it begins: 'Our Father in
heaven ...' *Father*! What an amazing beginning. It
conjures up – or should conjure up – the thought
of tender, loving care. You see, God is not just a
Creator who creates something out of nothing:
He is also a Father – with a father's love for
His children.

Jesus knew, however, that for some the word
'father' would have little meaning, or even a
negative connotation; they might not have had
a *loving* father and so there would be no loving
content in the word. So He adds another perspective by
talking about a man who came to his friend at midnight
and asked for the loan of three loaves. See how Jesus,
through carefully chosen words and phrases, builds up a
picture of God – a God who is both a *Father* and a *Friend*.
It is as if He is saying: 'If you have any problems about not
receiving the things that you feel you ought to be receiving,
then understand that the problem is not on God's side: He
is a loving Father and a concerned Friend.' If we don't get
this right, then we won't get anything right. Prayer that
doesn't begin here doesn't begin.

FURTHER STUDY

Psa. 103:8-22;
1 John 1:1-4

1. How does God feel about us?

2. Why did John write his letter?

**My Father and my God, I see that unless I begin right, I cannot
expect to finish right. Once again I ask You to give me an even
clearer and sharper vision of Your willingness and eagerness to
give. In Jesus' name. Amen.**

'How much more ...'

FOR READING & MEDITATION - ROMANS 8:28-39

'He who did not spare his own Son ... how will he not also,
along with him, graciously give us all things?' (v.32)

We continue our search for answers to the problem of why God sometimes withholds from us the very things He encourages us to pray for – things which we know for sure are in line with His will. We have seen that the reason is not because God is mean or tight-fisted. Jesus told us that God is both a loving Father and a concerned Friend. So let there be no doubt about it – God loves nothing better than to give good gifts to His children.

Let's read again the way Jesus puts it: '... how much more will your Father in heaven give the Holy Spirit to those who ask him' (Luke 11:13). Note the words – '*how much more*'. What gives an earthly father more delight than to be able to give to his children something he knows will be good for them and bring them pleasure? It is the same with our heavenly Father – *only a million times more*.

FURTHER STUDY

1 Chron. 29:10-16;
1 Kings 3:5-15

1. What did David acknowledge?

2. What surprised Solomon?

An old lady in a church I once had the care of approached me and asked for my help in 'straightening out' her prayer life. She told me that she never got any answers to her prayers, and when I asked her to tell me how she understood prayer and what sort of picture she had of the God to whom she was praying, she said: 'I picture God standing in the midst of heaven with His hands behind His back, and it is my job, through prayer, to try to get behind Him, prise open His hands and wrest from Him the things I need.' Can you understand how difficult it would be for a person like this, with such a warped concept of God, to approach Him with confidence and trust? She wasn't praying to God – she was praying to a caricature.

Father, it is clear that the way I see You will determine the way I approach You. Cleanse my mind and my heart of any misconceptions and misunderstandings that may be within me. Help me to see, Lord – really see. In Jesus' name. Amen.

FOR READING & MEDITATION – MATTHEW 7:1-12

'Ask and it will be given to you; seek and you will find;
knock and the door will be opened to you.' (v.7)

Now that we have cleared away any doubts about God's willingness and eagerness to give, we must go on to ask another important question: if God is such a joyous giver, why is it that so often we ask but do not receive? Isn't it true that sometimes we pray for things that are valid and legitimate – like a deeper encounter with the Holy Spirit – and life stays pretty much the way it is. We ask God to speak to us, but no answer is given. Why? I believe the answer lies in these words of Jesus: 'Ask and it will be given to you; seek and you will find; knock and the door will be opened to you' (Luke 11:9).

It seems to me from what Jesus is saying here that there are three aspects of spiritual longing and desire – asking, seeking and knocking. The usual interpretation of this text is that if, after we have asked, we do not receive, then we must become more intense and determined in our praying – and *seek*. Then, if after having intensified our praying, we still have not received, we must become still more intense and determined – and *knock*.

I wonder, however, whether Jesus was thinking here, not so much of intensity of action as intensity of desire. You see, prayer is not so much the words that cross our lips as the desire that is in our hearts. Some have such deep spiritual desires within them that all they need do is ask – and they receive. Others use all the right words and phrases, but their real desire does not match their words. Thus they have to go down to deeper levels of searching until they find the place where the desire of their hearts matches the prayer of their lips.

FURTHER STUDY

1 Sam. 1:1-20;
1 Kings 18:41-46;
James 5:17-18

1. How did Hannah express her desire to God?

2. What was significant about Elijah's way of prayer?

Gracious and loving Father, bring me to the place where my desire to receive is as strong, as Your desire to give. Then I know that 'all things are possible'. In Jesus' name I pray. Amen.

How deep is your desire?

FOR READING & MEDITATION - JEREMIAH 29:1-14

'You will seek me and find me when you seek me with
all your heart.' (v.13)

We ended yesterday with the challenging thought that
our ability to receive from God is not determined by
the prayers of our lips alone, but by the depth and degree
of spiritual desire we have in our heart. Listen to our text
for today in the Amplified Bible: 'Then you will seek Me,
inquire for and require Me *as a vital necessity* and find
Me; when you search for Me with all your heart'. It is that
principle – the principle of deep longing and desire – that I
believe links the three stages of prayer as outlined by our
Lord in Luke 11:9.

**FURTHER
STUDY**

Dan. 9:1-19;
Rom. 8:26-27

1. How did
Daniel show
his desire
when reading
Jeremiah 19?

2. How may the
Spirit move us?

I sometimes think that the Church has missed
its way in relation to its understanding of spiritual
desire. We mistake desire for demand, and this is
why we tend to see prayer as making demands
upon God rather than laying hold on what He
delights to give in response to our spiritual desire.
There is a place for asking in prayer, of course,
as the great prayers of the Old Testament show,
but prayer is more than a demand – it is also a
desire. And when our desire to receive matches,
even only feebly, God's desire to give – then the
sky's the limit.

Some Christians see in the words 'ask', 'seek' and
'knock' the thought that we must 'pound down' the gates
of heaven with our petitions in order to overcome God's
reluctance. They see God in the same way as the woman I
talked about the other day – standing in the midst of heaven
with His hands behind His back, waiting for His children
to wrest His answers from Him. Others, however – and I
hope you are one – see prayer, not as overcoming God's
reluctance, but laying hold of His highest willingness.

**Loving heavenly Father, I ask once again that You will help me
deepen my spiritual desire. For I long that my desire to please You
will be as strong as Your desire to please me. I yield myself to that
purpose. In Jesus' name. Amen.**

Inner - not outer

FOR READING & MEDITATION - MATTHEW 5:1-16

'Blessed are those who hunger and thirst for righteousness,
for they will be filled.' (v.6)

We spend one last day meditating on the thought that when our desire to receive matches God's desire to give – then the sky's the limit. We began a few days ago by saying that sometimes God withholds from us the very things He encourages us to pray for – things we know for certain are part of His purposes.

In seeking to understand God's reasons for doing this we have looked at the words of Jesus in Luke 11, where we saw that if we are not receiving the spiritual blessings that God has for us, then the fault is not in God. He not only gives – but *delights* to give. It is His nature to be large-hearted and magnanimous. If we ask and do not receive, it can only be that our heavenly Father perceives that the desire of our hearts does not match the words of our lips, and He will therefore withhold His blessings from us in order that we might go down into deeper levels of spiritual intensity.

But remember, the intensity He is looking for is not intensity of action, but of desire – not outer action but inner action. It does not mean that we have to shout and rave in order to get God to hear us, for He has already told us that He *delights* to give. It means, rather, that when we ask and do not receive, we should examine ourselves to see whether the desire of our hearts matches the desire of our lips. If it doesn't, then we must examine and intensify our spiritual desires at a deeper level of seeking. And if still nothing happens, then we go even deeper – and knock. This process is our heavenly Father's way of making sure that we learn not to take things for granted.

FURTHER STUDY

Luke 18:9-14;
James 4:1-3;
1 Pet. 3:7

1. Why did the Pharisee not receive from God?

2. What may hinder prayer?

O Father, I see that behind all Your withholdings is a desire for my spiritual maturity – so that my longing to receive matches Your longing to give. And help me learn never to take things for granted – but with gratitude. Amen.

Heaven on earth

FOR READING & MEDITATION - GENESIS 28:1-22

'How awesome is this place! This is none other than the house of God; this is the gate of heaven.' (v.17)

We continue our meditations on 'The Ways of God'. Another intriguing characteristic of our heavenly Father is *the way He has of revealing Himself through the most ordinary means and in the most unexpected places.*

The reading before us today helps to bring this thought into clear focus. Jacob had deceived his father and robbed his brother and, having obtained both the birthright and the blessing, he made his way to his uncle's home to find a wife. Three days after leaving Beersheba, he came to the hills of Bethel and, as it was evening, he settled down to

FURTHER STUDY

Judges 6:11-24;
Matt. 3:1-6

1. In what circumstances did Gideon experience God?

2. Why did people in Jerusalem prefer the desert to the Temple?

sleep. Then he dreamed a dream. He saw a ladder reaching from the ground up into heaven, on which angels were going up and coming down. In the dream God spoke to him – just as He had spoken to his father Isaac – a gracious, forgiving, personal, promissory word. Then, as the grey dawn crept around the sky, Jacob awoke with a great sense of awe and cried: 'Surely the LORD is in this place, and I was not aware of it' (v.16).

It is clear that when Jacob lay down to sleep, he had no expectation of meeting God. The stirrings of his conscience, which he had tried to stifle, had the effect of pushing God out of his thoughts. And besides, whoever would expect to meet God out there on the bare and barren hillside? Yet that was the place where God came to Jacob. On the basis of this, I want to put before you the thought that God constantly seeks to meet us in the common and unexpected places of life. He does not wait for what some call the 'high and intense moments', but makes the ordinary and the commonplace into the grand. Galilee and Glasgow are just the same to Him.

O Father, forgive me that I look for You only in the 'high moments' – and therefore miss what You might be saying to me in the ordinary moments. Take me deeper into this 'way' of Yours – and teach me more. In Jesus' name. Amen.

Cover to Cover Complete
– New NIV Edition

Back in 2007, CWR published *Cover to Cover Complete*, a Bible-reading plan with a difference. With the full Bible text in chronological order and daily features, this compelling resource took readers on a year-long voyage of discovery through God's Word, encountering the action in the order it happened.

The bestselling *Cover to Cover Complete* is now available in the updated New International Version, which was released in 2011.

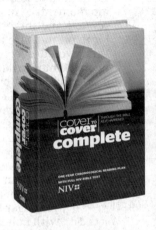

* Charts, maps and illustrations to enhance your understanding
* A timeline on every page, keeping every event in context for you
* Devotional thoughts for each day from Selwyn Hughes and Trevor Partridge
* The complete NIV (2011 edition) in chronological order, divided into manageable daily sections
* An accompanying section on the CWR website, featuring character studies, readers' testimonies, helpful hints and much more ...

Cover to Cover Complete NIV
ISBN: 978-1-85345-804-0
Introductory price
£21.99 until 31 December 2012.
RRP £24.99

Unexpected places

FOR READING & MEDITATION - GENESIS 18:1-14

'The LORD appeared to Abraham ... while he was sitting at the entrance to his tent in the heat of the day.' (v.1)

Some people find it difficult to believe that God can come to them in the commonplace of life – they expect to see Him or hear His voice only in the 'high or mountain-top moments' – moments that are filled with high spiritual content and intensity. But, as we saw yesterday, God met Jacob on the bare and barren hillside and under the stars. Who would ever expect to meet God in a desolate and unfrequented wilderness, where worship is unknown and it is unhallowed by praise? Yet it was there that God met and fought with Jacob. I am convinced that although God's prime way of meeting us is in and through the Scriptures, He is also constantly seeking to meet us in the common and unexpected places of life – through ordinary things and ordinary moments. And if we are not prepared for this, we can miss many a moment of spiritual discovery.

FURTHER STUDY

Exod. 3:1-12;
Mark 1:14-20;
2:13-14

1. Where did God call Moses?

2. Where did Jesus call some of His disciples?

I remember on one occasion standing in Trafalgar Square in London, when it was crowded with holidaymakers and visitors. I certainly never expected to hear God speak to me there – yet He did. That day the well-known fountains that are in the square were dry due to a failure of the pumps, and as I looked upon the scene God said to me: 'This is how your life will become unless you maintain constant contact with Me.' From that day to this, I have tried to keep my heart open to everything that is around me – and my life has been all the richer for it. As these lines say, to the discerning eye –

'Earth's crammed with heaven
And every common bush afire with God.'

Elizabeth Barrett Browning (1806–1861)

O Father, while not ceasing to search for You in Your Word, the Bible, help me to discover You also in the ordinary and the unexpected moments of life. Make the commonplace glorious for me today. In Jesus' name I pray. Amen.

Mingling with earthly clay

FOR READING & MEDITATION – MATTHEW 13:44-58

'Isn't this the carpenter's son?' (v.55)

The thought we are pursuing at the moment – that God is constantly seeking to meet us in the common and unexpected places of life – will, I know, present a problem to many. Some will say that the only place we find God is in Scripture, and outside that one and only infallible source, any revelation of God must be treated with suspicion and distrust. I have much sympathy with that line of thinking, for I know many who have sought to find God in the ordinary and the commonplace, only to come out with some of the strangest and weirdest interpretations of God and His ways I have ever heard. We must watch that we do not interpret Scripture by life's circumstances, but interpret life's circumstances by Scripture.

Having made that point clear, let me go on now to say once again that it is in our spiritual interests to develop an awareness of God in the ordinary and the commonplace. George MacDonald said: 'It is so easy to deny the nobility of something just because it mingles with our earthly clay.' How true – and when we do that we miss part of the meaning of the Incarnation.

Listen to the way one teacher makes this same point: 'When God came to earth in the person of His Son, He came as no hermit dwelling in a solitary place and giving Himself at rare intervals only to the few; He was born into the intimate home life of an ordinary family in Nazareth. When His ministry began, He kept Himself for the most part in the crowded ways of men; He dressed as they dressed, spoke with a Galilean accent, knew hunger and heartache and weariness and shared their life in everything but sin.'

FURTHER STUDY

Job 12:7-10;
Matt. 6:26-31;
Heb. 2:9-18

1. How may nature teach us spiritual truths?

2. What do we have in common with Jesus?

Lord Jesus, I am so grateful that while never ceasing to be what You had always been – true God – You became what You had never been before – true Man. You are as wonderful in Your humiliation as You are in Your exaltation. Amen.

The ordinariness of Jesus

FOR READING & MEDITATION – JOHN 14:1-14

'Don't you know me ... even after I have been among you such a long time? Anyone who has seen me has seen the Father.' (v.9)

We said yesterday that it is easy to deny the nobility of something just because it mingles with our earthly clay. Nowhere is this thought more clearly illustrated than in the passage before us. Philip seemed completely to miss the fact that the One with whom he had rubbed shoulders for so long was, in fact, God of very God. Just think of it – he asked God where God could be seen.

Some people come down hard on Philip for this, but consider the facts for a moment. Philip, no doubt, had been steeped in the traditional Jewish belief that God was

FURTHER STUDY

Gal. 4:4-5;
Phil. 2:5-11

1. What is ordinary about Jesus?

2. What is extraordinary about Him?

One, that He dwelt in some far-off splendour and that no man had ever seen His face. When he made his request, 'Lord, show us the Father and that will be enough for us', he probably had in mind the experience of Moses and believed that God could be seen only in some dazzling vision. Perhaps he hoped that Jesus would reward them with a similar experience and that their doubts would be shrivelled up in a dramatic and glorious encounter with the living God.

It is not surprising to me that Philip failed to recognise Jesus as God, for human nature is always more attracted to the spectacular than the truly great. If God had come to earth in a chariot of fire, multitudes would have knelt before Him. If He had moved among men with a shining face and dazzling apparel, He could have subdued kingdoms. But He was born as we are born, and His coming was noticed only by a few. When He grew up, He walked and worked in the dress of a common carpenter, and so blended the extraordinary with the normal that only the few saw that the extraordinary was there. Oh, the ordinariness of Jesus!

Lord Jesus Christ, Your ordinariness staggers and overwhelms me. The fact that You are God become Man is beyond my comprehension. Yet though I cannot understand it, I stand on it. Thank You, dear Saviour. Amen.

A day of decision

FOR READING & MEDITATION - JOHN 14:1-14

'... anyone who has faith in me will do what I have been doing.
He will do even greater things than these ...' (v.12)

It was because Jesus intertwined the commonplace with the glorious and came along a frequented path that so few were able to recognise Him. The unusual and ostentatious is always more attractive than that which is truly grand.

A pastor tells how, one evening, he stood with a group of friends waiting for a firework display to begin. While they waited, he turned and saw behind him a most glorious sunset. He said to the others: 'Look at that beautiful sunset.' But nobody looked. They were more interested in watching for a common squib. God came to earth unspectacularly and, despite the beauty and perfection of His life, He passed unrecognised in the midst of men. God was with them – and they sought Him afar. As we saw, even one of His own disciples asked Him where God could be seen.

There are many making the same mistake today. They are seeking at a distance the God who stands before them at the door of their heart. They are wondering how to ascend the ladder that reaches from earth to heaven and are waiting for it to be thrown down to them while, in fact, the foot of that ladder is right beside them.

Those of you who are Christians will bear with me, I know, if I pause to ask those reading these lines and who have never committed their lives to Jesus to reach out to God. The ladder is at your side. Ask God to come into your life, to forgive your sin and make you His child. Take my word for it – all you need do is reach out to Him. He will do the rest. Receive Him now – today.

FURTHER STUDY

John 1:1-18;
14:21-23;
Rev. 3:20

1. How has Jesus made God known?

2. How do we receive Christ?

O God, I have looked for the ladder of salvation to drop out of the skies, yet now I see it is at my side. I have looked for You afar off, yet You have been so near. I reach out now – with all my heart. Save me. In Jesus' name I ask it. Amen.

If you have made a decision for Christ today and would like a free copy of *Every Day with Jesus for New Christians*, please write to Mick at the address on the title page of these notes.

Ordinary words

FOR READING & MEDITATION - ACTS 10:1-23

'... the Holy Spirit said to him, "Three men have come to see you.
Go down and meet them ..."' (vv.19-20, TLB)

Not only does God involve Himself in the ordinary moments and the ordinary circumstances of life, but there are times when the words He speaks to us seem ordinary too. I was brought up to believe that if ever God spoke to me, He would do so in the language of the King James Bible. That is why the first words I ever heard Him say to me came as a complete and utter shock. I was staggered by their ordinariness.

Permit me to tell you about it. I had been a Christian only a few months and, one day, while kneeling in prayer at a Holy Communion service, I was pondering on how much Christ meant to me. As I waited, I heard God's voice ring out inside my soul: 'And you, my dear Selwyn, mean much to Me.' The words were very ordinary – no 'thee's' or 'thou's' – but I have no language to describe the effect they had upon me. The fact that God had spoken to me in ordinary words reached deep into my heart and mind. I confess that the very memory of that event is causing a tear to trickle down my face as I write.

FURTHER STUDY

John 2:1-11;
Acts 8:26-39

1. How did the ordinary servants become part of a miracle?

2. How did Philip lead a stranger to Christ?

The great Baptist preacher C.H. Spurgeon was fond of quoting the story of his housemaid, who told him that on the first day she began to work for him, she knelt by her bedside and dedicated her household duties to God. When she had finished her prayer, God spoke to her and said: 'Remember to sweep under the mats.' Oh yes, it is ordinary – absurdly so. But then God is concerned with ordinary things. Duties matter to Him. In the common moments of the day, God is there. Don't search afar; don't wait for some blinding vision. Look for Him in the ordinary ways of life. He is nearer to you than you think.

O Father, help me to make the most of every moment by seeing and sensing that You are in every one of them. Show me how to walk down familiar pathways and see unfamiliar things; to discover You in the ordinary and the mundane. Amen.

FOR READING & MEDITATION - ECCLESIASTES 9:1-10

'Whatever your hand finds to do, do it with all your might ...' (v.10)

We spend one last day meditating on the thought that God reveals Himself, not only in the sublime but also in the simple; not just in the extraordinary 'moments' of life but in the ordinary moments too. It's the way our heavenly Father likes to do things, and when we fail to understand this, we will deprive ourselves of many spiritual discoveries. So let me encourage you, as I encourage myself, to cultivate the view that sees God in ordinary things. Some of you are expecting a blinding revelation of God to come to you in the future – and it may well happen – but don't focus so much on what may lie ahead that you miss what God is doing in your ordinary moments now.

FURTHER STUDY

1 Cor. 10:31;
Col. 3:12-24

1. What should motivate all our activities?

2. How should we approach our everyday ordinary lives?

I read somewhere an old legend of an angel who came one evening to the edge of a river and asked the boatman to ferry him across. When they reached the farther shore, the angel rewarded the boatman with what appeared to be a handful of wooden shavings. In disgust, the boatman threw them into the river. The next morning he found one of those shavings left in the bottom of his boat and, on examining it closely, found it was not a shaving of wood at all but a shaving of gold.

My friend, the ordinary moments of life pass quickly – don't see them as worthless shavings to be thrown away in pique at receiving nothing better. Look at them more closely, and you will see that they are solid gold, for –

If on our daily course our mind
Be set to hallow all we find
New treasures still of countless price
God will provide for sacrifice.

John Keble (1792-1866)

O God my Father, now that I have caught something of the way in which You delight to invade the ordinary, help me to look more closely at my ordinary moments. For only then will I see that they are made, not of wood, but of gold. Amen.

In His time

FOR READING & MEDITATION - ECCLESIASTES 3:1-15
'He has made everything beautiful in its time.' (v.11)

What more can we learn about our heavenly Father's wondrous ways? This – it is His way *to finish and perfect everything He begins.*

Our text for today sums up that truth most beautifully when it says that He makes everything beautiful in its time. Notice the last three words – 'in its time'. Some things on which God is working may not look very beautiful at the moment, but they will – in time. A hymn Christians used to love to sing, born out of the verse that is before us today, says:

FURTHER STUDY

Ezek. 31:3-9;
2 Pet. 3:3-13

1. What made the cedar beautiful?

2. What is one reason for God's patience?

A time of rest will come to hearts grown weary,
A time of praise to those that grieve and sigh,
A time of joy to those whose lives are dreary,
The Lord's good time is coming by and by.

Jessie B. Pounds (1861–1921)

What needless suffering and anxiety we carry within us because we fail to understand that although God dwells in eternity, He is working out His purposes here on earth in accordance with time. He could bring about major changes in our lives in a single moment – and of course He often does – but usually His way is to work painstakingly through dark and difficult situations – taking His time.

A wise man once said: 'The greatest lesson we can learn from life is that God is never in a hurry.' I agree. He is the most patient in the universe. Believe me, we will save ourselves a good deal of personal pain and irritation when we learn to have patience with the patience of God.

My Father and my God, You are so poised, so persistent, so patient. It is Your way. I see that Your long-range purposes take time. Help me to be as patient as You are in waiting for them to come to pass. In Jesus' name. Amen.

Right on time

FOR READING & MEDITATION – PSALM 31:1–24
'My times are in your hands …' (v.15)

We quoted yesterday the words of a wise man who said: 'The greatest lesson we can learn from life is that God is never in a hurry.' And if we don't learn that lesson, we leave ourselves open to a good deal of irritation and frustration.

An example of how slow and unhurried God is in working out His purposes can be seen in Jesus' first advent. The promise that one day God would send someone to overturn the effects of the Fall was, as you know, given to Adam and to Eve in the Garden of Eden (Gen. 3:15). Later it was reiterated in many different ways – through the prophets, through the patriarchs, through the tabernacle and Temple sacrifices and so on. Century after century rolled by – and still no clear answer. 'Give us a Christ', cried out the masses of humanity as they sensed their need of someone to right the world's wrongs. But the heavens remained mute and silent. 'Give us a Christ', cried the nation of Israel as they saw the stones of their beloved Jerusalem overturned. But century after century came and went – and still no Christ.

FURTHER STUDY

John 11:1–45

1. Why did Jesus not hurry to be with Lazarus?

2. What was the result of His delayed arrival?

Then, when it looked as if God had forgotten His promise and no prophet had spoken in Israel for 400 years, the heavens responded and a Word was spoken – *Jesus*. A little bundle of life moved in a crib in Bethlehem and the greatest mystery of the ages took shape – 'the Word became flesh and dwelt among us'. Did Jesus arrive too late? Some might think so. But what does the Bible say? 'But when the time had fully come, God sent his Son …' (Gal. 4:4). He came not too early, not too late – but right on time.

Gracious and loving heavenly Father, You have made me in such a way that I can only give myself wholly to someone I trust. And if I cannot trust You – then who can I trust? You have my life – help me to trust You more. Amen.

God our comfort

FOR READING & MEDITATION - JOB 28:12-28

'God understands the way to it and he alone knows where
it dwells ...' (v.23)

How much we miss when we fail to see and sense God's
timing in our earthly affairs. If we look at our lives
strictly as they are laid out before us and lose sight of
the fact that God is at work, we can fall prey to doubt and
disillusionment. How often have we heard people say, when
things just don't seem to be working out, 'I find it difficult to
believe there is a loving purpose at work in my life. If there
is, then why do things take so long to come together?'

H.G. Wells once declared, in a wild and bitter mood, that
if there were a personal God behind this shambles of a
universe, he would spit in His face! It is easy to toss
that statement aside and regard it as blasphemous,
but I have sat with many committed Christians
who have gone through one tragedy after another,
and though they would not have used the words of
H.G. Wells, they certainly shared his sentiment. A
man I once knew very well and whom I regarded
as a fine Christian stood up in my presence and
shook his fist at God, saying: 'God, You don't know
what You are doing.'

FURTHER STUDY

Gen. 24:1-67

1. Find examples of God's perfect timing in this story.

2. Contrast the attitudes of Abraham and his servant.

What can save us from falling into such black
moods and using words of such defiance and
doubt? I know of nothing more effective than the
conviction that He makes everything beautiful in its time.
The picture you see now as you look at your life may not
be very beautiful, but when you see it through His eyes,
in His time, the picture takes on a perspective that is just
out of this world. You may begin to see purpose in tragedy,
reason in calamity and meaning in everything. No matter
what your circumstances, never, never lose hope. God is
our ever-present help and comfort.

**O Father, You know how easy this is to say, but how hard to hold
on to when I am hurting. Yet I know it to be true. I acknowledge
my need for greater dependency upon You. Help me, dear Lord. In
Jesus' name. Amen.**

Making all things work

FOR READING & MEDITATION – ROMANS 8:28

'And we know that in all things God works for the good of those who love him, who have been called according to his purpose.' (v.28)

The verse before us today is, as long-time readers of *Every Day with Jesus* know, a favourite of mine and they expect me to comment on it from time to time. If I was asked to give the two texts of Scripture that God has used most in my life, this would be one – the other being John 3:16. The key phrase in this verse is 'work together'. The verse is careful not to say that *all* things are *good*, for quite clearly, all things are not good. Sin is not good. Death and bereavement are not good. An earthquake or a flood is not good. All things are good only as they work together for God's purpose.

FURTHER STUDY

Rom. 5:1-5;
Phil. 1:12-21

1. What does suffering produce?

2. What was the result of Paul's suffering?

Some time ago, while in the United States, I drove past a college in Richmond, Virginia, and I remembered reading the story of a professor there who was asked by his students after he had addressed the morning assembly on the theme of Romans 8:28: 'But, Professor, you don't really believe that all things work together for good – all the pain and misery – do you?' The professor replied: 'The things in themselves may not be good, but God can make them work together for good.'

That afternoon, he and his wife were out driving when they collided with another car. His wife was killed instantly and he himself was left paralysed. One day, several weeks later, he sent for the president of the college and said: 'Tell my students that Romans 8:28 still holds good.' When, just one year later, the professor died, his students had the verse inscribed on his tombstone. At the ceremony, a local newspaper reporter asked them why they had done this. They replied: 'It was inscribed in his convictions: why not on his gravestone?'

O Father, I see that if I can have this truth inscribed in my convictions, then I will be able to face everything that comes with fortitude and faith. So, day by day, burn these words more deeply into my spirit. In Jesus' name I pray. Amen.

FOR READING & MEDITATION - 1 CORINTHIANS 2:6-16

'No eye has seen, no ear has heard, no mind has conceived what
God has prepared for those who love him ...' (v.9)

We continue meditating on the fact that it is our Father's
way to finish and perfect everything He begins. But
He does this over a period of time. Ah – there's the rub.
Some of us wish God would hurry up with His plans and
not take so long to get them accomplished – especially
when those plans cross and conflict with our personal
aims and desires.

If you struggle with the truth of God's timing, then
here's something you have got to get hold of – you may
not live to see God's time completely fulfilled. You may
live beyond the allotted threescore years and
ten, attain many of your personal goals and
ambitions and yet die before the completion of
God's purposes. But His promise stands – He will
make everything beautiful in its time. You see,
our problem is that we get our attention focused
on the wrong things. We see the strange-looking
cocoon; God sees the finished butterfly. We see
the ugly strands; He sees the finished design. We
see today – He sees tomorrow.

**FURTHER
STUDY**

2 Sam. 12:15-23;
Acts 7:54-60

1. How did
David's eternal
perspective
help him cope
with tragedy?

2. How did
Stephen cope
with his own
murder?

Let the text from Ecclesiastes that I have
given you over these past few days – 'He makes
everything beautiful in its time' – sink deeply
into your spirit. In my Bible, I have underlined the
word 'everything'. I believe God would not have
said 'everything' unless He meant everything. This means
that all your losses, failures, brokenness, heartaches, fears,
childhood hurts, fragmented dreams, lost loves, financial
reverses, sickness and illnesses will be made beautiful in
time. Without God, life is pointless and purposeless; with
Him, it will ultimately make complete sense.

**Dear, loving heavenly Father, I am thrilled beyond words to
realise I am caught up in something that has a cosmic guarantee.
Everything that has happened to me will be made beautiful in its
time. Hallelujah!**

Influences live on

FOR READING & MEDITATION - HEBREWS 11:1-16
'And by faith he still speaks, even though he is dead.' (v.4)

We stay with this thought that we may not live to see God's timing completely fulfilled. During the 18 years I spent as a pastor, I had occasion to witness the death of many Christians. Sometimes I would be called out in the middle of the night just to hold their hand and read to them from the Word of God as they passed into the presence of the Lord.

Often they would say to me: 'But there are so many things I have left undone. I wish God would give me a few more years to complete some of the things I want to do for Him.' Then I would read to them the text I have been bringing before you during the last few days: 'He makes everything beautiful in its time.' I would say something like this: 'The work you have started will not end when you die. It will still go on and God will see that it will be finished. He is not limited by your crossing over into His presence. The things that have happened to you will be taken by Him and woven into His glorious pattern so that when you see it in eternity, you will realise that it is our Father's way to finish and perfect everything He has begun.'

FURTHER STUDY

Matt. 26:6-13;
2 Cor. 4:17-18;
Heb. 11:27

1. How do the actions of a long-dead woman still speak to us?

2. Why should we try to see the unseen?

I hope the words that brought comfort to them will bring comfort to you now – especially those of you who feel that your life's work is coming to an end. Has life sped by so quickly that you feel there are many things left undone? Are you somewhat saddened when you think that the sand in the hourglass is running out? Then take heart – God will finish and perfect everything He has started in your life, even if He has to extend the influences of it into the next generation.

O Father, what delight and comfort it brings me to know that when my life here on earth ends, You will go on working on what I started and will not stop until You bring it to perfection. I am so grateful. Amen.

Death cannot cheat Him

FOR READING & MEDITATION - PHILIPPIANS 1:1-11

'... he who began a good work in you will carry it on to completion
until the day of Christ Jesus.' (v.6)

We spend one more day examining the thought that it is our Father's way to finish and perfect everything He begins. Everything God does is detailed and thorough. He does nothing with shallowness or superficiality. God is not interested in glueing onto our lives the thin veneers that are so typical of much modern furniture. He carves things that are solid and permanent – things that will outlast time and live on through eternity.

Charles Swindoll put it like this: 'Everything God does is thorough. It's never too little, never too late ... it's never too much, never too early and there's never anything missing.' So drop your anchor down deep into the thoroughness of God. Father God is going to do a complete and perfect work in your life and He will not allow anything, not even your death, to hinder Him. I have known many people, and I am sure you have too, whose lives still go on speaking and working for God long after they have passed on. It is as if God says: 'I am not able to perfect My purposes in this life over the period of one generation, so I need to extend them into another.'

I am thinking, as I write, of a friend of mine, now with the Lord, whose life seemed to consist of one failure after another. Yet amazingly, those failures drew his family together in such a way that out of them came a dedication and commitment to Christ that brought two sons into the Christian ministry and put a daughter on the mission field. I dare to believe that in eternity, the picture my friend will see is not one of failure but success, for He makes everything beautiful in its time.

FURTHER STUDY

1 Chron. 28:1-19; 29:1-5; Psa. 23:1-6

1. How did David's influence live on?

2. How does it still live on?

My Father and my God, I bow in adoration before the wonder of the fact that what You start, You finish - even if You have to go on working beyond death to complete it. Accept my deepest gratitude, dear Father - from the bottom of my heart. Amen.

God *insists* on it

FOR READING & MEDITATION – ISAIAH 42:1-16

'I will not give my glory to another...' (v.8)

We come now to the final section of our meditations on 'The Ways of God'. The point we have been making all through this issue is that the more we know and understand the ways of God, the less frustrated we will be when His ways interact with ours.

Some of the ways of God that we have discussed over these past weeks, we saw in operation during the acquiring and remodelling of Waverley Abbey House – particularly the revealing, reversing and restoring process. Had we not been given insight into this particular aspect of our heavenly Father's ways some years earlier, I suspect we would have experienced much greater anxiety than was the case.

FURTHER STUDY

Acts 12:18-24;
14:8-16;
2 Cor. 3:7-18

1. Contrast Herod and Paul.

2. What can we reflect but not possess?

The last 'way' of God we examine comes out of our text for today; it is the way God has of *ensuring that all the glory is given to Him.* I must confess that at one time, this particular aspect of God used to trouble me greatly. We all tend to despise those people who, having been involved in some achievement, want to hog the limelight and are unwilling to share the credit with others who have also had some part to play in it – even if a small one.

Had not God taught me and my colleagues the reason that lies behind Him wanting *all* the glory, then having reached the stage of completion of the remodelling process and the opening of Waverley Abbey House, we might have found ourselves vying with Him for acknowledgement and attention. There was no conflict, however, and it is with the greatest joy that we ascribe to Him *all* the honour, glory and praise.

Gracious and loving Father, I am so thankful that I am finding Your Way amid our ways. Daily, weekly, it is being disclosed before my eyes. Help me to know and understand You, for the more I know You, the more I will love You. Amen.

FOR READING & MEDITATION - REVELATION 5:1-14

'To him who sits on the throne and to the Lamb be praise and
honour and glory and power, for ever and ever!' (v.13)

We saw yesterday that if we do not understand why God insists on getting all the glory and honour for Himself, then we may find ourselves vying with Him for honour and attention.

Many Christians have stumbled over this aspect of God – the great writer C.S. Lewis among them. He says in one of his books that when he first began to draw near to belief in God, he found it difficult to understand why He insisted on being continually honoured and praised. He wrote: 'It was hideously like saying: "What I most want is to be told that I am good and great."'*

He went on to say that there were certain texts in Scripture, particularly in the Psalms, which seemed to suggest that those petitioning God were caught up in a kind of bargaining relationship with Him which proceeded along these lines: 'Lord, You do this for me, and I will give You the glory that You seem to find such delight in receiving.' Here's one such text, for example: 'Help us ... for your name's sake' (Psa. 79:9).

C.S. Lewis came to see that this was not the case, but it goes to show how easy it is to misunderstand and misinterpret Scripture when we fail to see the reasons that lie behind God's ways. Over the next few days, we shall explore together some of the reasons why God insists on taking the glory for Himself, but before we get to them, let's pause once again to recognise and deal with this terrible tendency we have to judge and interpret God's ways in the light of our own. For nothing could be further from the truth.

FURTHER STUDY

Psa. 96:1-13;
Rev. 19:5-8

1. How do we ascribe glory to God?

2. Why should we ascribe glory to God?

Gracious Lord and Master, You have made me in Your image, but so often I try to make You in my image. Help me once and for all to stop looking at Your ways in the light of my ways, but instead look at my ways in the light of Yours. Amen.

*C.S. Lewis, *Reflections on the Psalms* © copyright C.S. Lewis Pte Ltd 1958.

Worthy of all honour

FOR READING & MEDITATION – HEBREWS 1:1-14

'... sustaining all things by his powerful word.' (v.3)

We come now to face the question: why does God insist on taking all the honour and glory to Himself? Firstly – because He has a right to it. Can anyone deny Him that? God is not just the originator of our universe, but, as our text for today shows, He is constantly at work supporting and upholding it. And what a universe it is! Our scientists tell us that in relation to the myriads of other orbs that are in space, the earth on which we live is like a single grain of sand among all the other grains of sand *on all the sea-shores of the world*. They further tell us that if our earth

FURTHER STUDY

Psa. 8:1-9;
Col. 1:15-20

1. Why should we consider the universe?

2. What did Paul explain?

were to fall out of its orbit and spin away into space, it would make no more impact than the dropping of a pea into the Pacific Ocean.

Why am I using these word pictures? To show you that the God who created all this is a great and mighty Creator. Conceivably the world might have been constructed on a lesser scale. God could have designed just one solar system – and the universe would still be immense and amazing. The fact that He made it as large as it is points to the greatness of His mind and the greatness of His power in bringing it into being.

What is it all for? What purpose does it serve? To what does it point? It points to the fact that God is almighty and all-sufficient. This one fact alone ought to be enough to convince us that He has earned the right to unceasing honour and eternal praise. Everything we have – breath, life, reason and so on – we have received from Him. Dare we take any of the credit for the creation? Or give the glory to any other but our great and glorious God?

My Father and my God, You will have no argument from me. Help me at this very moment to focus all the appreciation that resides within my heart and direct it towards You. I honour and revere You, dear Father – more than words can convey. Amen.

'Day and night they never stop saying: "Holy, holy, holy is the Lord
God Almighty ..."' (v.8)

Another reason why God insists on us bringing to Him all the honour and the glory is this – the more we do this, the more we complete ourselves. Forgive me for taking you through what might be for some a complex train of reasoning, but I promise you, the effort you put into grasping the point I am making will bring its own spiritual reward.

Imagine a person standing in front of a beautiful painting or an exquisite piece of art and saying to themselves: 'My, this is an admirable piece of work' – what do they mean? They mean it deserves admiration, and that admiration is the only correct, adequate and appropriate response to it. But then someone like myself comes along, who has little experience or interest in pieces of art, and I simply glance at it, yawn and pass on.

FURTHER STUDY

Isa. 40:18-31;
Acts 17:21-34

1. What did Isaiah emphasise?

2. What problem did the Athenians have?

The person who is riveted to the spot by the beauty of the piece of art looks at me in amazement and says: 'Don't you appreciate what is before you?' I say: 'I'm afraid I don't really see much in it.' The person then replies: 'If you cannot see the genius in this, then there is a world you know nothing about – you are not fully awake. And with all your experience of people and of writing, there is a part of you that is incomplete. Not to appreciate what ought to be appreciated will leave you inwardly deprived.'

I would have no difficulty in accepting that argument, for although I have little personal interest in objects of art, I know intellectually that not to appreciate something that deserves to be appreciated results in some loss to me. In failing to honour God as God, I do not just deprive Him, I also deprive myself.

O Father, thank You for showing me that it is only when I focus on celebrating Your worth that I come awake. Help me always to be ready to ascribe to You all honour and glory, for I see that the more I do that, the more awake I shall be. Amen.

It is so right

FOR READING & MEDITATION – PSALM 92:1-15

'It is good to praise the LORD and make music to your name,
O Most High ...' (v.1)

We must dwell a little longer on the thought that one of the reasons why God insists on us giving Him honour and glory is because He knows that by so doing, we complete ourselves. C.S. Lewis articulates this thought far more effectively than I ever could when he says: 'He [God] is that Object to admire which is simply to be awake, to have entered the real world; not to appreciate which is to have lost the greatest experience and, in the end, to have lost all.'* A closely reasoned and complex statement but one well worth meditating on in your mind through the spare moments of this day.

FURTHER STUDY

Psa. 147:1-11;
Eph. 5:19-20;
Phil. 4:4-6

1. Why is it good to praise God?

2. How can we avoid anxiety?

He goes on to say that the lives of those who can't enjoy music, or who have never been in love, never known true friendship, are somewhat incomplete, and that this is a faint reflection of a life in which there is no attempt to live for the glory of God. I urge you to take hold of this thought, for once you see that the reason why God insists on you giving Him all the honour and glory is not that you might gratify some appetite in Him, but rather that *you* might become more whole and complete, then never again will you want to draw back from giving Him what He asks.

I have met many Christians who secretly thought that the text: 'My glory I will not give to another' implied that God is a Being who craves glory in the same way that some vain person searches for compliments or a new author sends his books to people who have never heard of him. But that, as you know now, is not His reason – He desires it, not just because it is right for Him, but also because it is right for us.

O Father, not only is it good to give You honour and praise – but it feels so right. Somehow everything within me is drawn towards health as I focus on giving You the glory You deserve. I am so thankful. Amen.

*C.S. Lewis, *Reflections on the Psalms* © copyright C.S. Lewis Pte Ltd 1958.

FOR READING & MEDITATION - ISAIAH 43:1-7

'... everyone who is called by my name, whom I created for
my glory ...' (v.7)

We look at yet another reason why God insists on us giving Him the glory – that in commanding us to glorify Him, God is inviting us to enjoy Him. The Westminster Catechism says that man's chief end is 'to glorify God and enjoy Him forever'. Fully to glorify God is fully to enjoy Him, and fully to enjoy Him is fully to glorify Him.

Follow me carefully at this point: if we could perfectly give glory to someone or something, that is, utterly express or get out the upsurge of appreciation that rises within us, then indeed the object would be fully appreciated and honoured and, in the giving of that honour, our own delight would attain perfect development. And the worthier the object, the more intense this delight would be. If it were possible for us in this present state perfectly to focus on and perfectly to delight in giving God the honour and glory which He deserves, and to keep this up moment by moment, then we would experience a peace and contentment that could not be described in words.

FURTHER STUDY

Matt. 5:1-16 (NKJV);
1 Cor. 6:20 (NKJV)

1. How can we glorify God?

2. How can others come to glorify God?

This is perhaps the closest we will ever get to imagining what heaven is like – a state and a place in which those who have been saved focus on bringing glory to the everlasting Creator and in so doing they experience in themselves perfect blessedness and contentment. Meanwhile, here on earth 'we are tuning our instruments in anticipation of the perfect symphony'. The tuning up of the orchestra can itself be a delight, but only to those who can in some measure anticipate what is to follow. Believe me, our glorifying of the Lord here on earth is but a trickle compared to the full flood that will flow out of us when we see Him face to face.

O Father, my heart longs for the day when I can give You perfect honour and praise. Meanwhile, help me to tune up my spirit, my instrument of worship, so that I shall be ready for the heavenly symphony. Amen.

'The family style'

FOR READING & MEDITATION - PSALM 18:20-32

'As for God, his way is perfect ...' (v.30)

We end our meditations where we began by affirming that without a knowledge of our Father's ways, we can soon find ourselves overcome by worry, frustration and fear. The eight ways of God around which this milestone issue has been built are, however, only some of our Father's special characteristics. He has many others.

Let me bring the ones that have occupied our attention in these meditations before you once again in the form of a final review. It is God's way (1) to train before He entrusts; (2) to reveal, reverse and then restore; (3) to place us in situations where everything seems to go wrong; (4) to arrange for some problems to be overcome quickly, but others to be overcome slowly; (5) to withhold from us the very things He encourages us to pray for; (6) to reveal Himself in the most ordinary of ways and in the most unexpected places; (7) to finish and perfect everything He begins; and (8) to insist on having all the glory for Himself.

FURTHER STUDY

2 Sam. 22:17-34;
Rom. 12:1-2

1. What did David declare about God's ways?

2. How can we know God's perfect will?

Knowing and understanding these ways of God will acquaint you with our heavenly Father's way of doing things. Then, at some time in the future, when you come up against a 'way' of God that seems strange and mysterious, you will be able to rest in Him and say to yourself: 'I know enough about my Father to realise that when I cannot see or understand the reason for His actions, He is pursuing a way that makes perfect sense.' You will find, as I have found, that it is not easy to lose in the dark the principles you have discovered in the light.

My Father, I am grateful for all I have learned about You and Your ways during these past days and weeks. Help me to carry these thoughts with me into the future so that never again will I be at the mercy of circumstances. In Jesus' name I ask it. Amen.

ORDER FORM

4 EASY WAYS TO ORDER:

1. Phone in your credit card order: **01252 784710** (Mon-Fri, 9.30am - 5pm)
2. Visit our Online Store at **www.cwr.org.uk/store**
3. Send this form together with your payment to:
   CWR, Waverley Abbey House, Waverley Lane, Farnham, Surrey GU9 8EP
4. Visit your local Christian bookshop

For a list of our National Distributors, who supply countries outside the UK, visit www.cwr.org.uk/distributors

YOUR DETAILS (REQUIRED FOR ORDERS AND DONATIONS)

Name:	**CWR ID No.** (if known):
Home Address:	
	Postcode:
Telephone No. (for queries):	**Email:**

PUBLICATIONS

TITLE	QTY	PRICE	TOTAL
		Total publications	

All CWR adult Bible-reading notes are also available in ebook and email subscription format.
Visit www.cwr.org.uk for further information.

UK p&p: up to £24.99 = **£2.99**; £25.00 and over = **FREE**	
Elsewhere p&p: up to £10 = **£4.95**; £10.01 - £50 = **£6.95**; £50.01 - £99.99 = **£10**; £100 and over = **£30**	
Please allow 14 days for delivery Total publications and p&p **A**	

SUBSCRIPTIONS* (NON DIRECT DEBIT)

	QTY	PRICE (INCLUDING P&P)			TOTAL
		UK	Europe	Elsewhere	
Every Day with Jesus (1yr, 6 issues)		£15.50	£19.25	Please contact nearest National Distributor or CWR direct	
Large Print *Every Day with Jesus* (1yr, 6 issues)		£15.50	£19.25		
Inspiring Women Every Day (1yr, 6 issues)		£15.50	£19.25		
Life Every Day (Jeff Lucas) (1yr, 6 issues)		£15.50	£19.25		
Cover to Cover Every Day (1yr, 6 issues)		£15.50	£19.25		
Mettle: 14-18s (1yr, 3 issues)		£13.80	£15.90		
YP's: 11-15s (1yr, 6 issues)		£15.50	£19.25		
Topz: 7-11s (1yr, 6 issues)		£15.50	£19.25		
Total Subscriptions (Subscription prices already include postage and packing) **B**					

Please circle which bimonthly issue you would like your subscription to commence from:
Jan/Feb Mar/Apr May/Jun Jul/Aug Sep/Oct Nov/Dec

* Only use this section for subscriptions paid for by credit/debit card or
cheque. For Direct Debit subscriptions see overleaf.

CONTINUED OVERLEAF >>

PAYMENT DETAILS

☐ I enclose a cheque/PO made payable to CWR for the amount of: **£** _____

☐ Please charge my credit/debit card.

Cardholder's name (in BLOCK CAPITALS) _____

Card No. ☐☐☐☐ ☐☐☐☐ ☐☐☐☐ ☐☐☐☐

Expires end ☐☐☐☐   Security Code ☐☐☐

GIFT TO CWR

☐ Please send me an acknowledgement of my gift   **C** ☐

GIFT AID (YOUR HOME ADDRESS REQUIRED, SEE OVERLEAF)

giftaid it

I am a UK taxpayer and want CWR to reclaim the tax on all my donations for the four years prior to this year **and on** all donations I make from the date of this Gift Aid declaration until further notice.*

Taxpayer's Full Name (in BLOCK CAPITALS) _____

Signature _____   **Date** _____

*I understand I must pay an amount of Income/Capital Gains Tax at least equal to the tax the charity reclaims in the tax year.

GRAND TOTAL (Total of A, B, & C) ☐

SUBSCRIPTIONS BY DIRECT DEBIT (UK BANK ACCOUNT HOLDERS ONLY)

Subscriptions cost £15.50 (except *Mettle*: £13.80) for one year for delivery within the UK. Please tick relevant boxes and fill in the form be

☐ *Every Day with Jesus* (1yr, 6 issues)
☐ Large Print *Every Day with Jesus* (1yr, 6 issues)
☐ *Inspiring Women Every Day* (1yr, 6 issues)
☐ *Life Every Day* (Jeff Lucas) (1yr, 6 issues)

☐ *Cover to Cover Every Day* (1yr, 6 issues)
☐ *Mettle*: 14-18s (1yr, 3 issues)
☐ *YP's*: 11-15s (1yr, 6 issues)
☐ *Topz*: 7-11s (1yr, 6 issues)

Issue to commence fro
☐ Jan/Feb ☐ Jul/Aug
☐ Mar/Apr ☐ Sep/Oct
☐ May/Jun ☐ Nov/Dec

CWR

Instruction to your Bank or Building Society to pay by Direct Debit

DIRECT Debit

Please fill in the form and send to: CWR, Waverley Abbey House, Waverley Lane, Farnham, Surrey GU9 8EP

Name and full postal address of your Bank or Building Society

To: The Manager _____ Bank/Building Society

Address _____

_____ Postcode _____

Originator's Identification Number

4	2	0	4	8	7

Reference

☐☐☐☐☐☐☐☐☐☐☐☐☐☐☐☐☐☐

Instruction to your Bank or Building Society

Please pay CWR Direct Debits from the account detailed in this Instruction subje to the safeguards assured by the Direct Debit Guarantee.
I understand that this Instruction may remain with CWR and, if so, details will be passed electronically to my Bank/Building Society.

Name(s) of Account Holder(s)

_____

Branch Sort Code

☐☐ ☐☐ ☐☐

Bank/Building Society account number

☐☐☐☐☐☐☐☐

Signature(s)

_____

Date _____

Banks and Building Societies may not accept Direct Debit Instructions for some types of account